10 Things I Hate About My Husband

How God healed my heart, restored my marriage & set me free

Shayla Huber

10 Things I Hate About My Husband | Shayla Huber

For more information, please contact: connect@shaylamariehuber.com

Book cover Design: *Shelby Walls*
Editor*: Stephanie Miller (http://www.butterfly-beginnings.com)*
Copy Editing, layout & format*: Chelsia McCoy/Your Writing Table (www.yourwritingtable.com)*

Dedication

For all of the women who married
their Prince Charming...
but haven't made it to the fairytale yet.

Your Happily Ever After Awaits.

Table of Contents

Foreword
Written by Heather Shriver Burns

My journey as a mom of three, wife, and teacher turned CEO has been full of twists and turns, high and lows, and mountain top and valley moments that have stretched me beyond measure. While we don't always understand the "why" in the thick of hard things, God is faithful and does what He promises to do. He turns all things to good for those who love Him. I'm going to assume you picked up this book because you're ready for more good in your life and you're really ready for more good in your marriage. I want to be the first to congratulate you on investing in yourself and your marriage. It's an intimate topic not many people are willing to talk honestly about. That's one thing I love about Shayla. She's willing to talk about the hard things.

I don't know about you but what I've found to be true is that the seasons of pursuing more good things can feel really stinking hard. Roadblocks tend to pop up left and right out of nowhere. But when we have faith that better is possible and give God our "yes," He leads us to the holy things that transform us in ways we never could have imagined. I've had the honor of walking through hard and holy seasons with hundreds of women just like you, pursuing more of God and more good in their lives. One of those women I've had the pleasure of walking with is Shayla, first as her business coach and then as a friend.

As a Master Coach and mentor for Kingdom entrepreneurs, I have the honor of creating space for women to be honest about what they really want and what they really believe so they can make the necessary changes and take the necessary steps to achieve their heart's desires. As you read each chapter of this book, ˈou will get the same opportunity to get honest with yourself about ˈt you really want and what you really believe so that you can ˈ your heart's desires for your marriage.

ˈur life is a reflection of your belief system. That includes ˈ. Thankfully, Shayla's taken the first step to expose ˈemy in her belief system and is as vulnerable as one can be throughout this book. Each chapter is an invitation for you to do the same. Will it be easy? No. Will it be worth it? YES!

Many women have been conditioned to be strong and independent and sweep their feelings under the rug. What I love about this book is that it won't allow you to do that. Shayla knows your marriage is too important, your family is too important, and you are too important. Each chapter exposes the lies that have robbed Shayla of a joy-filled life and joy-filled marriage so you can get a head start in the areas God wants to show you where the enemy has stolen, killed, or destroyed God's perfect plans for you.

They say hurt people hurt people. I can bet you've experienced that to be true in your life. But what I also know to be true is loved people love people, healed people heal people, and free people can't help but want to free others. The book you have in your hands is the result of Shayla's healing, love, and freedom journey with the Father. Each page is the result of her saying "YES" to the hard and holy work required to get to her "Happily Ever After."

As a coach, I'm so proud of her for giving God her "yes" and writing this book when it was the last thing she saw coming. As a sister in Christ, I am so excited for you and so many other women to be able to read her testimonies of transformation so you know you're not alone and you know there is hope for your heart's desire to live out God's best for you and your marriage, too. If you're ready to do the hard and holy work that brings long lasting change, it's time to turn the page and pursue your "Happily Ever After."

Heather Shriver Burns
Founder, Seek First CEO ™
Master Coach, Speaker & Podcast Host

But whenever someone turns to the Lord, the veil is taken away. For the Lord is the Spirit, and wherever the Spirit of the Lord is, there is freedom. So all of us who have had that veil removed can see and reflect the glory of the Lord. And the Lord - who is the Spirit - makes us more and more like him as we are changed into his glorious image.

2 Corinthians 3:16-18 (NLT)

Introduction:
This Ain't Your Grandma's Marriage Book

I'm just going to come right out and address the elephant in the room, friend. As of right now, I am a 33-year old wife and mom to two boys, ages 5 and 2. I'm sure you might be thinking I am totally unqualified to be writing a book about marriage based on the fact that I don't have years and years of experience under my belt. I've got seven to be exact. But what I lack in years, I make up for with growth, transformation, and relatability. I'm in the trenches now. Right now. I'm growing a business, raising my boys, and trying to support my husband all at the same time. I'm dealing with bills, laundry, supper, ranch life, dirty diapers, and Paw Patrol just like you. I have those days where it seems like from sun-up to sun-down all I do is fetch granola bars and fruit snacks, break up fights, and fold the never ending pile of laundry.

I'm in the season of life where most marriages begin to dissolve because who has time for romance when all the responsibilities of life are closing in on you? My brain is so overloaded sometimes with planning meals, cleaning the house, trying to be a kind and gentle mom (despite raising absolutely wild boys), and also maintaining and growing my coaching/mentorship business, with an active social media presence. If you've ever felt like you couldn't handle one more thing on your plate or you were going to snap like a twig, then sister, you are not alone.

Trust me when I say, I see you. I know your innermost frustrations. I know how annoyed you get when your husband comes home from working all day and instantly takes his spot in his chair to decompress. I know how hurt you feel when he doesn't ask you how your day was. I know the anger that creeps in when it feels like he doesn't appreciate all you do for your family and home. And I also know the face you make when he asks you where the remote is while you are literally balancing a baby on your hip, cooking supper, and talking on the phone to your mom all at the same time. *How dare he ask me for anything right now*, you think to yourself. *Doesn't he even notice how busy I am right now?* I can already see the death glare shooting his way and the shrug of his shoulder saying, "Geez what's your problem?" And that's why I'm the one who is supposed to write this book. Because I get you. And that death glare – ah I know it well. I used to wear it every day myself. However, it's been gone for quite some time now, and replaced with a much sweeter look. One that is full of compassion, love, and grace.

As I sit here, in my new cozy little ranch house overlooking a beautiful yard where my boys can run and play and run free, I am reminded just how far my husband, Cody and I have come to get to this place. I can remember the old, run down rental we lived in when we got married, the secondhand table we sat at when we ate our "one year anniversary" cake, and the conversations we had about starting a family that were equal parts terrifying and intoxicating. But I also remember the feel of that front door I slammed in his face countless times, the hoarseness of my throat from screaming so loud at him, and the countless late nights I spent alone because he was out of town. I type the words "10 things I hate about my husband" as the title of this book, and I am filled with complete awe to know that how I once felt about my husband has been replaced with so much goodness and love that I don't even know what to do with it all. When I say this is a total redemption story, I am not playing around!

Now, *hate* is a strong word, and I never actually hated my husband, Cody. I love him with all my heart. And those who know him, know how incredible he is. He would do literally anything for anyone; and he is a great husband and father. But all those annoying things he did, like never picking up after himself or leaving his dirty clothes right next to the hamper, all those times he didn't communicate well and expected me to drop everything I was doing in order to help him, all those times we were on different planets and couldn't seem to agree on anything, I hated it. It made me feel so frustrated. It made me question how in the world we ended up together. It made me feel like I was damaged goods because I know I married a great guy and why couldn't I just be happy? It made me wonder if anyone else ever felt the way that I felt and if this really was what marriage was like? You know, putting up with someone else's quirks for the rest of your life, and feeling misunderstood the majority of the time. *This was not what I signed up for.*

Especially as newlyweds, everyone on social media makes it look so perfect. You buy the house, you have the kids, you take the vacation and post all the Instagram worthy photos, but no one ever talks about the messy, ugly and hard. No one ever talks about the fights or how to figure out a budget. No one talks about how two individual people are supposed to merge their thoughts, ideas, backgrounds, values, and goals together. It's easier to talk about the good and gloss over the hard.

The world will tell you that this is just what marriage is like. Nowadays, marriage is talked about more in a joking manner than it is as a beautiful commitment to another person. Marriage is seen as disposable, instead of as something to be cherished and worked on and prayed over. It's not seen as something God intended to bring us joy and happiness and fulfillment. With the divorce rate being really high, the world tells us it's not that big of a deal, and we can leave at any time. When things get rough, it really is okay to either walk away or just stay married in misery as two independent people coexisting. Those are your two choices.

I see it differently, and as you will see soon — so does God. God designed marriage to be a holy and sanctifying process of two people coming together to become one, with the ultimate alignment to be the will of our Heavenly Father. And you want to know the opposite of holy? Common. That's right. Common. So, if you desire a kingdom marriage, one that will make you more holy and bring you the fruit of what God has promised you, then you can't have a common marriage. You can't do as the world does and expect a God-fueled marriage. This is one of the biggest revelations you will come to understand as you read this book, and I'm just getting started.

I'll be totally honest with you, you are either going to feel so seen reading this… or you are going to think I'm a complete nut job, pray for my husband and stop reading this book today! I mean, I titled this book "10 Things I Hate About My Husband" and that's a pretty bold move. But the redemption, the transformation, and the growth that has happened in my life and marriage as a result of God's grace demanded a bold title.

For those who are already vibing with me, keep reading because I'm going to show you how I went from sitting in a lot of anger, frustration, and emptiness when it came to my marriage (and honestly my life at times) to a place of acceptance, abundance, peace, and love. I went from hanging up the phone on my husband mid-call, giving him the cold shoulder when he walked through the door, and holding grudges for days, to forgiving him, serving him, and honoring him. Has it been easy? No. Has it been worth it? Yes. It has only been through taking a hard look at myself and letting God heal my heart that anything started to change in my marriage.

And before you think that this radical change is just for me, I'm calling you higher right now. I'm calling you to embrace a new understanding for your part in your marriage. I'm calling you to lay down your weapons, tear down the walls you've built up, and to take a deep breath for the journey to come. I'm calling you to release the tension that you've been holding onto for far too long, even though it seems like part of your day-to-day life at this point. Regardless of your situation, lack of trust, or history of past hurts and neglect—it's time to lay it down. For the sake of your marriage, it's time for a change. And that change starts with your relationship with Jesus.

Perhaps you may be feeling disappointed by my above declaration of what, or who is really responsible for saving your marriage. Maybe you picked up this book hoping it was a manual to help you change your husband. The easy button would be to take all of those annoyances and frustrations you have and tell your husband to figure his crap out and come find you when he does. *Either you change or I'm checking out.* How many other wives do you know that have threatened their husband in hopes that they would be forced to change? I'm guessing quite a lot.

I was that wife. The wife who couldn't wait to jump on the phone and vent my anger to anyone who would listen.

"I can't believe he can't put his dang clothes in the hamper."
"I can't believe he never asks me how I feel!"
"I can't believe he spent money without asking me."

And on and on and on! Cody, if you are reading this, please forgive me. My humanness was shining through and they are certainly not my finest moments.

Speaking of my husband, he is very aware of the content of this book and my mission to help wives in their marriages. He's been my biggest supporter and has continued to encourage me every step of the way, even as I share so candidly about our marriage in these pages. See, I told you he was a great guy!

Here I am, just laying it all out on the line. I truly can't believe I'm admitting this all to you right now. Sharing my deepest emotions is crazy uncomfortable, but I'm also choosing to believe that maybe, just maybe, there is one other woman out there who has felt the same way. The woman who has known deep anger and frustration, but at the same time knows her marriage isn't a mistake. She knows that there is something special between her and her husband and she is willing to learn and grow in order to find the peace that was promised to her on her wedding day. I'm talking to the woman who is yearning to find the holy part of marriage again, or maybe experience it for the first time. Deep down she knows her anger isn't really her husband's fault. Her anger is a deep wound in desperate need of healing. Yes, putting my marriage on display feels uncomfortable, but if it helps other women experience freedom in their relationships with God and their husband, it's well worth it.

I'm laying out 10 different issues that I struggled with in my marriage. Some are small. Some are big. Each of them depicts the lies that I believed from the enemy and the stories that I made up in my mind. They showcase how my childhood and my heart wounds projected in unhealthy ways onto my husband, causing more division and strife. And yep, you guessed it—they all have God as the main character of the story. He is there time and time again, picking up the broken pieces of my heart and teaching me what a healthy marriage should look and feel like.

In the beginning years, I would put a band-aid on these issues. As in, we're going to fight about this and then move on. For example, I would burst out in anger about Cody getting home late multiple nights in a row. We would hash it out until I felt like I had spoken my mind and then put a band-aid over the hurt only for it to surface again. *Just forget it so we can have a fun weekend,* I would tell myself. The problem with the band-aid is that we were on a rollercoaster of highs and lows and we never came to a meaningful resolution. Band-aids can be a great quick fix, but they are not meant to be a permanent solution.

As I matured a little bit and started on a personal growth journey, I began to at least put Neosporin on the band-aid. Instead of yelling and slamming doors because he was getting home late, I tried harder to understand my husband and respect the fact that sometimes 7:00 pm is the only time he has in the day to rope with help and maybe instead of stewing at home, I should just go to the barn and be with him there. My fellow wives of farmers/ranchers/ cowboys, God bless y'all!

Finally, as God began to change my heart and I developed a relationship with Him, He gave me the strength to reopen my wounds in order to have lasting healing in Him. I hated it when my husband got home late; not because I was a jealous or possessive wife, but because I had a wound of abandonment from childhood. It felt like such a big deal every single time Cody got home late because my heart was subconsciously remembering what it felt like to cry myself to sleep as a little girl, wishing I had more of my dad in my life. And as only God can do, He rewrapped and healed those wounds with love, care, and understanding.

Almost every harsh word spoken to my husband, every belief I had about not feeling loved by him, and the insecurities that came to the surface after getting married were all directly related to my heart. They were related to my past experiences of being neglected, pushed aside, and forgotten by people who were supposed to love me. I wanted my husband to love me perfectly, and when he failed because of his humanness—all hell broke loose.

At the end of the day, marriage is just two imperfect people who choose to love each other through the ups and downs of this life. Even still, there is so much more to that story that many people don't want to admit. The longer my heart wounds festered and bubbled without being treated, the more our day-to-day life was infected with misunderstanding, frustration, and the enemy's fiery darts. My hope and prayer is that through my story and revelations, you can head straight to deeper healing. You can skip all the tiny band-aids and go right to the part where God will reveal to you what heart wounds you still have and how he wants to heal it. You can start to pinpoint the lies that you have been believing about your own husband and marriage and why they seem to have such power over you. I believe you will start to understand the kingdom marriage God has planned for you, and despite how you were raised or what the world says about it, that kind of marriage can be yours. Because it's not so much about your husband and getting what you want. It's about rooting your identity in Christ and becoming more like Jesus and seeing what you can give. It's about letting God's love overtake you until there is nothing but overflow that comes out of you.

I'll just tell you right now. Before you read the rest of this book, you need to know something else about me. I'm not a "half in" person. I get something in my head and I tend to go all in. I don't want just a little piece of the pie; I want the whole dang thing. I don't want to be just an okay mom; I want to be the best mom I can be. I don't want an average marriage or an average bank account, I want abundance. So with that comes intensity. With that comes intentionality and nitty gritty growth and vulnerability. I have been assigned to speak boldly and directly to you about your marriage and I believe it will hit you in the best ways, out of love.

If you are here for all of that, and you are going to read this book with an open mind and heart, ready for the growth that it can bring, let's do this. I think this book is going to make you cry, laugh, think, and pray. It's going to bring you hope in places and humble you in others. I think it's going to allow you the time and space that you desperately need to look into your own heart to see what God wants to heal. To look at your marriage and be so full of gratitude and love for all that is still to come for you and your husband.

Imagine what it will feel like if instead of ignoring your husband when he gets home, you greet him at the door and you both chat about your day. Imagine what it will feel like to spend time together, not out of obligation but out of joy and want. Imagine what it will feel like to have a partner again and not just a roommate. Imagine what it will be like to pray and read your Bible together. All of that and more is inside of these pages.

A quick note about how this book is laid out. At the end of all the chapters, except for the first and last, there will be a prayer, a scripture, and question prompts for you to connect with. Feel free to make the prayer your own, put the scripture where you can see it daily, and answer the questions honestly. Maybe one of the ten topics will resonate with you more than the others. For example, the chapter about money may hit you in all of the right places, more than the chapter about intimacy. For these areas, I encourage you to focus on and consistently talk with the Lord about it and allow him to help you work through it. I've written this book with the goal of having each chapter build onto the next. So even if something feels like it doesn't perfectly apply to you and your specific situation, I promise as you continue to read, God will reveal those points that need attention.

My prayer is that my personal experiences and insights bring you clarity and hope in your own life and marriage. My heart is to see you claim your identity in Christ fully, so that the love you feel from Him flows into your family. My goal is to help you shut up the lies of the enemy once and for all so there is more peace and harmony in your home. No matter how lost, broken, or frustrated you are right now, let me walk alongside you to show you that there is beauty in the mess and there is purpose in your pain.

So here we go! 10 things I hate about my husband… let's start at the beginning.

1.
Cowboy Dreams

You know how they say you marry your dad? Not literally, but in the sense that your husband and your father share common interests or personality traits? Well, in my case, that's exactly what happened. As the daughter of a second-generation cowboy and stock contractor, I have rodeo in my blood and some of my best memories as a little girl were traveling all over the country with my family, putting on rodeos. I remember spending all of my time either running around with my cousins playing cops and robbers, or sitting with my grandma in the secretary's office coloring on back numbers and drawing pictures. We filled up on popsicles, Pepsi, and food from the hospitality tent back in those days and everyone pitched in during the rodeo. Everyone had a job and after the rodeo was over, we played even more in the arena until they turned the lights completely off.

Cody also has rodeo running through his veins and one of the most fascinating things about us (at least to me) is that our childhoods overlapped. His dad competed as a professional calf roper during that time and was at many of our family rodeos. While I was busy running around with my cousins and helping my grandmother, Cody was usually found with a rope in his hand, immersed with all the big cowboys. He never strayed far from his dad and was always at the roping chute, so he never really ran around with us crazy kids. And while I was able to stay at the rodeo for the whole weekend, Cody and his family were only there for a few hours and then they were headed to the next one to try and win some money. Needless to say, our paths did not cross much even though we shared the same location many, many times.

It wasn't until the summer of 2012 that we bumped into

each other at his high school rodeo finals. We had that awkward, "Hey! I kind of know you, how are you?" conversation to which I walked away from and thought nothing of it. I was entering into my senior year of college and not looking for a boyfriend. Romance just wasn't on my mind at that time—but I can't say the same for Cody.

When I got that Facebook friend request from him just hours later, it was clear that our bumping into each other meant more to him than it did me. I got that feeling that most girls get when you can just "tell" that a boy might be interested in you and sending a friend request right away just confirmed my gut feeling. But again, I didn't have time for a boyfriend, so I planned to ignore him all together.

And do you know what that sneaky cowboy did? He lied to me about his internet connection so I would give him my phone number! "Hey Shayla, I'm about to lose service on Facebook, here is my phone number. Text me if you want." Like, what would you do? I kind of felt like it was the nice thing to do, and I believed he didn't have the service… so I texted him.

I will never forget talking to my roommate at the time about our 3 year age difference and being super worried about it. I mean, don't get me wrong, cowboys are most definitely my type. What woman hasn't dreamed of a hunky cowboy sweeping them off her feet? But the age difference felt so big. He was just entering college and I was almost done. But he was so sweet, and my roommate said "why not?" So that was the beginning of us.

That summer we took advantage of every rodeo we were at together and got to know each other. It was most definitely a heart-racing summer and kind of felt like it was out of a movie. Cheering him on during the rodeo performances, walking around the carnival before they had to leave in the morning, sitting on the bucking chutes talking about anything and everything—we couldn't get enough of each other. I can remember the bright lights from the carnival rides, the music and loud laughter of the people at the dance, and the smells of the funnel cakes and corn dogs. Even though there were always so many people around when we were together, it felt like it was just us, in our own little bubble. It was a whirlwind of a summer, and we did everything we could to steal a few minutes alone. He knew how to make me feel special and I didn't want that summer to end.

I will never forget our very last date, that August before he was scheduled to leave. We spent the whole day at Adventureland, which is one of Iowa's biggest theme parks. Then we went to the Iowa State Fair and chose to spend a little bit too much time together that evening, if you know what I mean. But gosh darn it. We were falling in love and he was leaving to go to Texas for his first year of college and we wanted to make the day last as long as we possibly could. Even though we had only been dating for 3 months, we didn't want to face reality outside of that blissful summer.

Maybe my reminiscing makes you think of your first few dates with your husband. The newness, the excitement, the googly eyes, and how the both of you were on your best behavior during that time. The phone calls that lasted hours, the good night kisses, and the ache in your belly when you were apart. Let's just sit with those memories for just a second, shall we? Doesn't it feel kind of nice?

Okay, back to our love story. Even though he went to school out of state, we knew that we were going to try the long-distance thing. I went back to school for my senior year of college at Wartburg (Waverly, Iowa), where I was getting my education degree and Cody went off to Texas to rodeo for Vernon College and get his 2-year degree. During that time, we did everything we could to see each other. I remember flying to Oklahoma for one of his college rodeos and having to crash at my mom's friend's house because I missed my flight back home. And now I can't remember if that was on purpose or if the flight really did get canceled... again, we were in love. Don't judge me.

10 Things I Hate About My Husband

****

After six months, Cody just couldn't take the distance anymore (okay, I didn't like the distance either), so he transferred to Iowa Central Community College to be closer to home and to rodeo for the college rodeo team. With distance no longer an issue between us, we were together every weekend. We would stock the truck with candy and pop and spend the weekend driving to all of his rodeos. We loved every minute of it and it became apparent that we had found the person that our heart longed for. It wasn't just the excitement and the thrill of dating any more, it was the feeling of safety and comfort that we had with each other. We stopped trying to be what we thought the other person wanted and were able to be ourselves. The first time he told me he loved me (in that Oklahoma airport parking lot), I cried like a baby. And I wasn't even that embarrassed about it! Because my heart just knew that this love was real and that I had found the one.

Now, without having to relay all the details of those first few years together, just know, we were not perfect. There were some bumps along the way. We hurt each other, we made up, we did our best, and we loved hard (just like any other young couple). And on April 2nd, 2016, we officially tied the knot in a beautiful barn wedding near my hometown, with our closest friends and family there with us. It was my dream come true.

I wore a white lace dress and he wore his Cinch jeans, boots, cowboy hat and dress coat. We had the most beautiful cupcake display with rustic burlap and rope decorations. And under the arch that said, "What God has joined together, let no man separate," we said our vows and we promised to love each other forever. We tied three cords together to signify Ecclesiastes 4:9-12: "*A cord of three strands is not easily broken*" and it still hangs in our bedroom to this day. And as we danced the night away to "Copper Head Road" and "When Will I Be Loved" by Vince Gill, I was so excited for our life together and couldn't have been any more in love with my cowboy.

Shayla Huber

I was teaching school full-time by now, so I took a couple of days off and we headed to Kissimmee, Florida for Cody's RAM National Circuit Finals that he had qualified for back in November. While we were there, we went to Sea World and out to eat a few times and called it our honeymoon. The focus of the trip was the rodeo and I was perfectly fine with that. I knew what I was signing up for when I married a cowboy. Your life revolves around the rodeo schedule, and that means even your honeymoon!

Then we went home. Gosh, you know what they say, marriage changes everything. You get even more comfortable with each other, maybe even a little lazy. The phone calls are shorter and aren't so much to chat, but to simply make plans and figure out what's for supper that night. Date nights out on the town are replaced with binge-watching a TV show at home. The bathroom towels are thrown on the floor instead of always being picked up. The bills and responsibilities become a bigger deal and you are just trying to navigate it all.

And for us, a small town schoolteacher and a rodeo cowboy, bills were a big topic of discussion. I began supplementing my income through network marketing to work on paying off my student loan debt, and Cody was doing all he could to make ends meet too. It was a struggle, but we made the best of it. We knew in our hearts that the calling on our lives and using our gifts and talents meant more to us than making money any other way.

At least, that's what I told myself to make myself feel better. And that's what I led my husband to believe. I supported him, I enjoyed working hard at what I was doing, and together, we were "living the dream." On the outside, we both seemed to be pursuing careers that we loved, we had the means to live the rodeo lifestyle, and we seemed very happy. But deep, deep inside the recesses of my heart, I was starting to get annoyed and anxious. I was struggling with the feeling of not having enough and constantly worried we wouldn't have the money we needed to pay our bills.

10 Things I Hate About My Husband

Real life seemed to be smacking us in the face financially, and we were not prepared for it. Money consumed my thoughts and began to dictate all of our conversations. There was a discontentment growing inside of me, and as you will see next, it began to divide what God had brought together.

2.
Money, Money, Money

Alright sister. Raise your hand if you and your husband are on opposite ends of the spectrum when it comes to spending money. One of you balances the checkbook, the other one doesn't. One of you spends without checking the price tag, the other one only looks at the bargain bin. One of you thinks money grows on trees, the other one is a Frugal Frannie. Okay, you get the point I'm making, and whether you have a large bank account or a small bank account, one income or two— it really doesn't matter because money makes the world go round.

So, which one are you? In our household, I am the saver and Cody is the spender. And when you can't seem to agree with how your money is being spent, it can cause some heated arguments. The type of arguments when you can literally feel your body getting hot because your spouse spent money on something without asking you. And since he doesn't balance the checkbook, he has no idea if enough money was in there to cover the expense, so you will be the one trying to figure out how to pay the credit card bill.

It's these times when you're on different pages about how to handle money that seem completely overwhelming—even suffocating. There is a reason that they say money issues are one of the top five leading reasons for divorce in the United States. The bottom line is, you don't want money to control you any more— you want to be in control of your money. And you want your husband to feel the same way. Is that too much to ask?

I don't know about you, but I married for love. We were just living on love! We didn't exactly have an in-depth conversation before getting married about money management.

10 Things I Hate About My Husband

We believed we would always have enough money and if we needed more, we would just work harder. I think we just assumed that we were on the same page without actually having a discussion about it.

However, during those first couple years of marriage, the difference in how we viewed money started to rear its ugly head. It wasn't just what we spent money on, but also our habits and mindset around saving. I tracked every penny of our income and expenses, while Cody didn't. I started to get the itch to pay off my student loans which were around $30,000 and Cody didn't seem to care about paying off any kind of debt.

It became obvious to me pretty quickly that we were not on the same page. And as I realized I would be alone on this "debt-free" journey I had decided to embark on—I made the mistake to take things into my own hands. I decided that his money was his money and my money was my money and I would do what I needed to do to get my student loans paid off. So on my newfound quest, I joined my first network marketing side gig to do just that. Problem solved, right?! Wrong.

In true Shayla fashion, I dove right into this new world of social selling on a mission. I only saw green. Whatever I needed to do to make more money, I did it. I taught school during the day and sold Scentsy wax bars at night. With this side hustle, I was making a decent $500-$1,000 extra per month but it only made me hungrier for more. When I got wind of a newer company selling the latest and greatest hair care products, I decided to give that company a shot. *Maybe I'll make more money selling these products because no one around here has heard about them yet*, I thought. I started sharing these haircare products on Facebook and in person, and it blew up. I was selling so much that I also had recruited other women to start selling it with me. Suddenly, I was making more money than I ever had before and I was hooked. It felt like I had opened this magical door of never-ending money, and finally we had "enough." We could take a deep breath. With all of this momentum, I was able to pay those student loans off in no time. It felt easy. Too easy. So, I kept going.

And during all of this mass selling frenzy I found myself in—I was also pregnant. Even though I was busting my behind, it felt like everything was falling into place the way I wanted it to. I was making enough money to quit my teaching job and become a "work-from-home-mom." It just felt like all the stars were aligning perfectly for us. I loved every moment of it, and I thought that adding a baby would only make life sweeter.

On April 18th, 2018, exactly two years after we got married, our first baby boy entered our world. Leroy Kenneth Huber came unexpectedly 3 and a half weeks early, so I had no bags packed and no sub plans made for school. I'll never forget finishing my massive plate of left-over lasagna, standing up, and instantly being washed away with more water than I knew I could hold. I ran to the bathroom to transplant this waterfall somewhere and yelled for Cody to get his butt in the bathroom. "I think my water just broke!"

And in true husband fashion, Cody says, "So what do we do?!"

"I'm assuming we should pack a bag and get to the hospital," I said with a shaky and anxious voice.

As I watched my husband scrambling to pack a bag with sweatpants, nursing bras, and toothbrushes, I couldn't help but laugh. As scared as I was to think my baby was early—I was excited to start this new chapter of our life. I was ready to become a full-time mom, rest easy on the business foundation that I had built, and just enjoy life.

A few days later, we brought Leroy home to our first purchased house. It was small, cozy, and completely remodeled on the inside. There were no mice to deal with, no mold in the closets, and no landlord to pay like the last house we had lived in. It was ours. Have you ever had that moment in life where you feel like you have "made it?" That's pretty much how we felt. We had gotten through the broke newlywed phase and are now obviously well-equipped and "well to do" parents. And those opposite views on money? Well, the surplus of what I was making in my business was enough to ease all our worries and doubts.

We spent our first summer with Leroy rodeoing out west and created some crazy memories. I'll never forget the night a man high on something tried breaking into our truck in Casper, WY and the sight of five police cars swarming our truck while Leroy slept soundly in his car seat. Or the time we broke down on the side of Monarch Pass headed to a rodeo in Gunnison, Colorado. While Cody walked to get help, I got out my folding rocking chair and rocked my baby right there on the side of the mountain. Safe to say we haven't been back to that rodeo since, but the views were sure great!

Despite the craziness of it all, and being on the road with a 3-month old, we loved it. The cool morning mountain breeze and the hot afternoon sun. The all night drives and the gorgeous morning sunrises. The arenas with picture perfect backgrounds of mountain silhouettes in the distance. Very different from our Midwest rodeos. It was exhausting yet exhilarating. I loved supporting my husband and I was able to do some work from my phone during that time in order to keep up with my booming business. It was the best of both worlds, or so it seemed.

But as my business grew, so did my goals. It wasn't enough being able to pay off my student loans; I decided we needed to pay off the credit card debt, too. Oh, and we might as well get my car paid off as well because that will make me feel even more safe and comfortable. Why stop at making $10,000/month when I could actually make $20,000/month? Why not keep shooting for the stars and going big? My hunger for more was becoming insatiable. I didn't realize it at the time, but now looking back, I can see it for the obsession that it became.

I wanted more money because money felt safe to me. I wanted more money to prove I was worth something. I wanted more money to be able to live a life of freedom and to help Cody's dream as well. There is no getting around it… rodeo ain't cheap. You have feed bills, vet bills, entry fees, diesel, truck and trailer payments, and the list goes on and on. With rodeo, you have to pay to play. You pay an entry fee and if you don't place or win anything then you are just out that money. It's gone. And typically rodeo cowboys are traveling every single day, especially in the summertime. You will rope at one place, get in the truck, and drive to the next. It could be 30 minutes away, 6 hours away, or 12 hours away. There are thousands of miles put on the truck, and as you can imagine a massive diesel bill to match. Add in a horse to take care of, the cost of equipment, and food because you gotta eat… expenses add up quickly.

****

In the beginning, my intentions were so pure to try and release this financial pressure off of my husband. I never wanted to see him held back because of money. But my ultimate heart posture screamed a spirit of mammon. I was putting all of my faith and worship into a piece of paper that I thought could buy us happiness and everything we needed in the world. I felt like the more money I made, the happier we would be as a family. For those of you who aren't familiar with this term, "mammon" is a spirit that is connected to money/wealth and can influence people to trust the money more than they trust God.

I'm not gonna lie; more money did make us happy—for a time. Our reality was that when we had plenty of money, we were happy. So, I justified this need for more because if we are happy now, imagine what even more will feel like! And on the flip side of that, when we had a month where our income was lower than usual, stress set in. Panic ensued. We started fighting more because of the lack of resources. I was constantly caught up in the future, never feeling totally settled and thankful for what we did have. Talk about an exhausting way to live.

And there was one thing back then that I didn't do. I never

asked what Cody's financial goals were. I never asked him what he really wanted our bank account to say. I really didn't discuss any of it with him because it was "my" money. Remember? His money was paying his bills and rodeo expenses, and my money was paying the rest with any extra going towards credit card or car debt. I thought I was being so clever but had no idea what a slippery slope we were on by having our finances separated in this way. On our wedding day, we promised to become one before our Heavenly Father in all areas of our life, and yet we weren't acting like it in one of the most important factors in a marriage. Finances.

My internal need for more soon developed into resenting Cody for financial decisions he was making. I mean, the guy had the audacity to buy a $1.39 pop at Casey's almost every single day. And I was over here busting my butt to manage our money, pay off debts, and hustle in my business. I felt like he didn't see how hard I was working and was just spending money to spend money, while I was over here literally never spending a dime on myself… pinching every penny. And it drove me absolutely insane.

I was so obsessed with the idea of living a debt-free life, and the freedom that it would bring that his "reckless" spending, as I saw it back then, seemed totally unfair. I didn't understand how he didn't also see the benefits of living debt-free and the biblical principle behind it. It became something I was ashamed of and so if I had an extra $50, I put it towards paying our debt. I wasn't going to dare spend it on myself. My obsession was growing, yet it was poison for our marriage.

Money consumed my thoughts and dictated my every move. It drove my actions within my business to the point where I would stay up later, get up earlier, invest in more trainings -- all to figure out how to make more. I felt like I had to be on 24/7 with my business or I would lose everything. It took priority in my life; even over being a good wife and mom.

I'll never forget calling a friend of mine to seek help because the resentment I was feeling for my husband was choking me. This phone call was the first time I had called someone to seek wise, Godly counsel. Not to vent or complain. Not to unload my problems. But to seek some solutions. My friend had gone through a big rebirth in her own marriage and knew she would be a great person to talk to. I knew I couldn't keep operating like this. I didn't want to keep operating like this. I didn't want to keep fighting the same fight over and over and over. I didn't want him to keep looking at me like I was a crazy person. I knew what I was talking about; and he was choosing not to listen to me.

As much as I acted like it was my way or the highway, I so desperately wanted to be on the same page as him but I was going about it in all of the wrong ways. I condemned Cody for everything he bought, even something as small as a pop from the gas station! I was picking fights with every bill I looked at and remember literally seeing red because he did not appreciate or acknowledge the sacrifices I was making to help us get ahead.

But I had blinders on and I couldn't see all the other things he was doing, too. Even when he won a rodeo and brought money home, I was too focused on the money going out to pay any attention to how hard he was working. I hated the concept of "you gotta spend money to make money," and yet that was my husband's anthem. Will my husband ever follow the Dave Ramsey plan to a T? No, no he will not. And trying to get him to see it my way was only tearing us apart and making us both miserable in the process.

Remember those stress free days after Leroy was born and we seemed to be high on life? Those days were gone. And I so desperately wanted them back; but not at the expense of giving up this dream I had of living completely debt free. Not at the expense of having enough money in the bank to make me feel safe and comfortable. Oh no. Not at the expense of my love for money.

The more nagging, more fighting, and more talking I did about our money differences only produced more lack. More division. It felt like Cody was starting to build a wall around himself and the more I tried to take down that wall, the stronger he made it. He was sick and tired of talking about it and he sure let me know it. A phrase he continually used to say was, "All you care about is money." And as much as I tried to deny it, he was right.

I didn't realize it then, but now I do. The enemy had us right where he wanted us. He so desperately wants to divide marriages, cause chaos, and rip apart families because he knows how deadly a strong, God-fearing family is. He knows the power and holiness of a marriage sanctified by God and the glory it will bring to God's kingdom. Marriage is a pure gift from God and the devil will do anything to tear it apart, including using our own differences and beliefs to create confusion. John 10:10 says: "The thief comes to steal, kill, and destroy," and sister, our marriages are one of the first things he attacks.

He used my good intentions, my growth mindset, and my ambitions to create a wedge between my husband and me. The spirit of mammon became so loud in my head. This idea that money was the end all be all and we were not safe without it, that God's calming voice had no room at all.

Matthew 6:24 says: *"No one can serve two masters. For you will hate one and love the other; you will be devoted to one and despise the other. You cannot serve both God and money."* (NLT) All the bitterness and resentment I felt from being so different from Cody when it came to our finances ultimately was rooted in a deep heart issue that said, "God, I don't truly believe you are a good provider. I don't truly trust you to take care of my needs. I think earthly money is going to keep me safe and I know more about it than you do." *Ouch.*

Friend, this is a lie straight from the pits of hell, yet I believed it. I had no idea back then how engrossed I had become with this spirit of "mammon." I wouldn't have been able to even tell you the definition of it, which is when one's life becomes a quest to accumulate more and more wealth until it becomes an object of worship. It starts with a void that is present in your heart and grows when you try to fill that void with anything else but God.

For the sake of how this sneaky spirit can seep into your life, let's backtrack a little into my past. My parents got divorced when I was around 3 years old, and I lived with my mom, stepdad, brother, and stepbrothers. I would consider us a middle class family; meaning, sometimes we had more money, sometimes we had less. But I never felt like we were missing out on anything. Whether it was back to school shopping, traveling AAU basketball, or a beautiful prom dress my parents made it happen. When I decided to go to a private college, my mom got a second job just to help me pay for some of it. I was so grateful for everything and was taught that you work hard for what you have.

I got my first job when I was 14 years old, working at the local grocery store in the deli department. I remember playing my basketball games every Friday night and then waking up every Saturday morning for the 7:00 am shift at the deli, getting the donuts and coffee ready, making potato salad, and frying chicken for the lunch hour. It wasn't the most glorious job, but I truly loved greeting the grandpas of our little town who were there for their morning coffee. I remember one of them telling me that someday I was going to make a really great wife... Oh, if he only knew!

Eventually, I got sick and tired of smelling like fried chicken and waking up at the butt crack of dawn, so I got a job at the mall selling panties and underwear at "the bra store" as it was called. It was a much more sophisticated job for a 16-year old girl in high school and I loved it. I mean, I had a great employee discount, only had to drive about two minutes to get to work, and talking to people all day was right up my alley.

Once I decided that I was going to go to college to become a teacher, I then got a job working at one of the daycare centers in my town. I absolutely loved the preschool aged kids and after graduating from high school, I was off to Wartburg College for the next 4 years to major in Elementary Education. While there, I had multiple different jobs, a repeat of my high school experience. In many ways, work was all I knew and I always had a job.

After graduating college, I accepted a reading teacher position at Interstate 35 Community Schools. I'll never forget that interview, because as soon as it was over, I was changing out of my pencil skirt and hopping in Cody's pickup truck, headed to another rodeo. We celebrated with Dr. Pepper and Hershey's bars and I felt like the luckiest girl in the world. I was finally going to have a real, steady income, have my summers off, and do something that I enjoyed and had been preparing for!

When network marketing entered my life that fall, I wasn't necessarily looking to quit my teaching job. I just thought making some extra cash would be a great way to pay off my student loans. But when I started making double what I made in a month on a teacher's salary, it opened up a whole new world of possibility for me. It allowed me to see an opportunity to support Cody's career that didn't require me to work all of the time.

This was such a new concept to me! This girl who had had a job since she was 14 years old, had always pinched pennies and worked for every dime I had, and the thought of making money while I slept was intoxicating to say the least. It had a snowball effect on me, and as I explained earlier, the more success I had, the more I craved. The more obsessed I became with this vision of time and financial freedom. My circumstances were in complete control over my emotions, attitudes, and beliefs.

Before I knew it, I was not only putting pressure on myself to pay bills and pay off debt but I was carrying this invisible burden to help my husband accomplish his dreams, too. I was surrounded by women in business retiring their husbands and I wanted to do the same thing for Cody, except it looked more like funding his dream rather than quitting a job. The kicker is he never asked this of me. I just took on this role and when I didn't feel appreciated for it, that's when resentment kicked in. I believed that his dream would not and could not become a reality without me and my business success. This was the ugly story in my head that I could not shake.

So, in reality, my husband's spending habits were never the actual issue to our disagreements. It was a spirit of mammon that said, "God won't take care of you so it's all on you to figure it out." It was a lie from the enemy that made me believe money was the answer for happiness, fulfillment, and peace here on earth. It kept me focused on the future, instead of being able to enjoy today.

How many fights about money have you had with your husband because you felt like there wasn't going to be enough to pay the bills? How many nights did you lose sleep over unexpected expenses entering your life, like a new water heater or needing new tires on your car? How many times have you looked at other people on social media and been filled with envy because they seem to have more than you? How many times have you believed the lies whispered into your ears?

Trust me, I know how frustrating it is to have a different view on money than your husband. I know all of those times you tried talking to him about money to get him to see it your way, you had good intentions. But ultimately, when we place money above our husbands it causes division. When we place money over God, it's a sin that keeps us separated from Him. Why do we look to our abilities when God tells us that He is our perfect and ultimate provider?

In Luke 12:24-28, Jesus says: *"Look at the ravens. They don't plant or harvest or store food in barns, for God feeds them. And you are far more valuable to him than any birds! Can all your worries add a single moment to your life? And if worry can't accomplish a little thing like that, what's the use of worrying over bigger things? Look at the lilies and how they grow. They don't work or make their clothing, yet Solomon in all his glory was not dressed as beautifully as they are. And if God cares so wonderfully for flowers that are here today and thrown into the fire tomorrow, he will certainly care for you. Why do you have so little faith?"* (NLT)

10 Things I Hate About My Husband

The world is constantly going to be telling us that we need more. We need to keep up with the Jones'. That time and financial freedom is attached to our bank accounts, and not the freedom we get from having a relationship with Jesus. What God says is that we already have everything that we need! It's time to tune out the expensive enticements of the world and instead focus on growing in our life-giving relationship with God and doing what He has called you to do. More money is not the answer. More Jesus is.

After years of operating with the spirit of mammon and fighting with my husband about money, God showed me that it was never going to bring me safety or happiness. My income had gone up and down more times than I could keep up with when I first entered the world of network marketing, and that was reason enough to see that God is the only constant in my life. When my focus turned to Him as my source and sustainer, the spirit of mammon lost all of its power over me.

If this resonates with you, you can repent and renounce the spirit of mammon once and for all. *"Don't store up treasures here on earth, where moths eat them and rust destroys them, and where thieves break in and steal. Store your treasures in heaven, where moths and rust cannot destroy, and thieves do not break in and steal. Wherever your treasure is, there the desires of your heart will also be."* (Matthew 6:19-21 NLT)

I am not saying that money is the root of all evil, but what I am saying is that the *love of money* is. And that's where I found myself and that is why it became such a monster in my life and marriage. I thought I was being mature and smart with my money by paying off debt, watching every penny, and working my butt off for more. Inherently, these things are not bad things. They become rotten when you value them over God's word and when you stop trusting in Him and his provision. They become rotten when you are valuing those things above your marriage. They become rotten when you aren't working as a team with your spouse to get your finances on the right path.

If money is one of the biggest things that is tearing your marriage apart… here are my suggestions:

1. Stop caring so much. Seriously. Just decide to stop caring about him buying the pop at the gas station. In the grand scheme of things, is it really that big of a deal? Not really. Again, your husband should be a higher priority than your finances. When I loosened the noose around my husband's throat about his spending habits, it actually helped the situation rather than made him go crazy with his spending. He started being more intentional with when and where he spent money and I think he was just thankful that I was off his back about it. I decided that if a pop at Casey's brings him joy, then more power to him! I also stopped depriving myself of so many things and allowed myself a treat every now and then, too. The Lord has shown me that it's okay to take this financial journey one day at a time. "*Give us today our daily bread.*" (Matthew 6:11 NLT) When you depend on Him to provide for your every need, the worry and stress disappear.

2. Communicate with each other! This is something that started happening very naturally when I really started to spend time with God. I'll be honest, though. It wasn't always easy. I still had days when I was doing bills and I could feel the pit in my stomach go hollow again because I wasn't quite sure where the money was coming from. But every month, we had enough. And in these moments, God reminded me of Luke 16:10: "*If you are faithful in the little things, you will be faithful in large ones. But if you are dishonest in little things, you won't be honest with greater responsibilities.*"

The Lord has shown me, through the ups and downs of my income, that I truly will not be trusted with more until I am faithful with the little. That created in me a spirit of gratitude and contentment and following His voice is ultimately what will bring the abundance He wants to give me. And as I started operating from this mindset, Cody and I began talking about our finances again. He started to see a change in me and that money no longer had its grip on me. This is a prime example of my actions, not my words, starting to impact my husband in a big way. We started to communicate about some things we could implement to pay off debt that would make sense for both of us, and not just benefit one of us. God started downloading strategies and opportunities that honored our marriage above either of our careers. He brought us to a point where we could grow together in a peaceful and loving way, instead of shaming the other for not thinking the same. And I believe this is the way that he always intended our finances to look like. Together.

Recently, Cody came home one night and told me about an opportunity to rope where his fees would be paid for. This means that the fees you would normally pay in order to enter the rodeo (which sometimes can be hundreds of dollars) were paid for! And this was actually the second opportunity he had that same month to rope, with very little expenses.

This little financial break could not have come at a better time. We were in the middle of remodeling his grandparents' farmhouse for us to move into and were about 1 month away from moving in. He was having some horse issues and things were just not where we wanted them to be. I could tell he was getting discouraged and down about it. It was on my heart to share Matthew 6:26, which is one of my very favorite verses of all time. *"Consider the birds - do you think they worry about their existence? They don't plant or reap or store up food, yet your heavenly Father provides them each with food. Aren't you much more valuable to your Father than they?"* (NLT)

I said, "Babe! God created you to rope. This is His way of providing a way for you when you really didn't see a way. You need to take this blessing." And of course, he looks at me kind of funny and shrugs his shoulders. But in my mind, I'm thinking "Believe me or not, that's my story and I'm sticking to it!" And I kid you not, the Holy Spirit was just showing up that night and five minutes later I went to put Leroy to bed and we opened up his Jesus Storybook Bible to the exact same story! I yelled into the kitchen and said, "See! I told you! It's confirmation that you need to go!" I even got a little smile out of him that time. I love when God works swiftly and boldly like He did that evening.

I have so many more stories tucked into my back pocket of the ways that God has now shown up in our finances since we started fully trusting Him. I know how easy it is to get caught up in the things of this world we can see. I mean this chapter shows you the mess I got myself in, but true faith in the unseen and taking God at his word has brought me a lot more peace and joy than I ever thought possible. I can't even begin to explain how it has helped Cody and I mend a broken piece in our marriage. At the end of the day, financial issues are often symptoms of a deeper heart problem that only God can fix.

God's abundance doesn't just come in the form of financial blessings, and when we get too caught up in that, we miss that his abundance can be found in every area of our lives! It's about our quality of life. It's about healthy marriages and homes. It's about the peace that he fills you with and the light he gives to you to share with the world. Remember the enemy who wants to steal, kill and destroy? Well God's purpose is to bring you a rich and satisfying life. In Him you will have more than you could ever ask for. Just like the birds and the flowers, God takes care of his loved children each and every day. Declare it and believe it today!

SCRIPTURE:
Deuteronomy 28:11-14 (NLT)
"The Lord will give you prosperity in the land he swore to your ancestors to give you, blessing you with many children, numerous

livestock, and abundant crops. The Lord will send rain at the proper time from his rich treasury in the heavens and will bless all the work you do. You will lend to many nations, but you will never need to borrow from them. If you listen to these commands of the Lord your God that I am giving you today, and if you carefully obey them, the Lord will make you the head and not the tail, and you will always be on top and never at the bottom. You must not turn away from any of the commands I am giving you today, nor follow after other gods and worship them."

PRAYER:

Father God, today, I ask for a fresh perspective over our financial life. I ask you to break any spirits or strongholds that may be keeping me from experiencing your true heavenly blessings. In the name of Jesus Christ, I ask for forgiveness for trusting in earthly possessions over your great favor. I'm sorry for making money an idol in my life in any way and I trust you completely for provision. This is your money. Help me to steward it well. Thank you for the gift of my husband, of the work we get to do, and the way you guide us in our finances. I love you and praise your holy name. Amen.

QUESTIONS:

1. What is a thought(s) that you believe about money?
2. What is the root of that thought?
    What beliefs were passed down to you?
3. Can you identify the differences between you and your husband's money mindsets and how it is causing division?
4. Where do you see God's blessings in your life, beyond financial?

3.
What About My Dreams?

So here we go! My Type A, strong-willed, and ambitious spirit is about to shine through here in this chapter. If you are anything like me, goal-oriented, and always looking to achieve, this might hit you square in the face. There is nothing wrong with being a go-getter. I think it's one of the reasons my husband fell in love with me in the first place, actually. And I don't want you to think for a second that the ambitions God gave you are a mistake. But man, when those ambitions are out of integrity with the word of God…it can be a recipe for disaster!

So, remember when I told you about my first teaching job? I absolutely thought it was what I wanted to do with the rest of my life. I loved it. And I loved the people and the kids I got to work with. But what I quickly realized being married to a rodeo cowboy was that he was gone. A lot. And as a teacher I couldn't exactly drop everything I was doing and go with him. Even though I was able to travel with him in the summertime for his big run, all those winter rodeos, finals that he qualified for, and ropings during the year? He had to go without me. And who wants to be left behind? Not me. I loved being able to go with him and it was lonely when he was gone. Any woman who is married to someone who travels a lot can definitely relate! Many weekends, when I found myself at home without Cody, I would schedule things into my calendar to make me feel less alone. And that's what led me straight into the world of network marketing.

One fall weekend, I had scheduled in to my (very busy) calendar a party at my friend's house. She said there would be someone there sharing these really cool, pleasant-smelling, wax warmers. I figured since I love candles, I bet I will love these too.

10 Things I Hate About My Husband

And I did! All the different variations of warmers and fragrances, the little catalogs you could flip through, and the cozy rich smell of fall wafting through the house captivated me. And the fact that the host of the party was able to earn free products just by referring her friends was such a cool concept!

As I went to place my order, I flat out asked the saleswoman if she made decent money selling this stuff. And come to find out, she did! I was bursting with excitement thinking of all the possibilities this opportunity had to offer. I'm not afraid to talk to people. I like parties. I love my house to smell really good. And if I could make money to put towards my student loans, sign me up! My wheels were officially turning and my eyes were opened to a whole new way of making money. But little did I know, this little side hustle was going to turn into something much, much more.

So here I am, hosting as many home parties and Facebook parties as I could. Selling wax and warmers to anyone who would listen to me. The more I hustled, the more money I made. I remember getting postcards in the mail from being the top enroller on my team and that motivated me so much. I loved being a winner. I loved accomplishing something. I loved making a goal and crushing it. But the feeling of accomplishment was short-lived, and I was on to the next big goal.

I started to understand this business model of network marketing and it just made sense to me. I enjoyed getting customers, but I became even more motivated to build a team, help others start a business, and experience the benefits of leveraged income. I was surprisingly very natural at it all. I was a schoolteacher, not a saleswoman so it caught me a little off guard. I would work all day at school, come home and host parties or sort orders. I was truly having fun and catching a bigger vision for my life.   Have you ever been in one of those situations where you are happy with what you have, but deep down you are still hungry for more? Whether it is eating a whole pan of brownies, binge

44

watching a TV show, or working on a project you just can't seem to stop? Well, that's pretty much how I was operating at that time in my life.

I enjoyed making the extra money, but I wanted more. I wanted more influence and status. I wanted more recognition. I wanted to be better than I currently was. I was introduced to the world of personal growth and development around this time and just wanted to grow. Don't get me wrong, I don't think there is anything wrong with growth or wanting to be better.

But as I'll explain soon, my hunger and need for more was actually rooted in low self-esteem. It was rooted in a way to prove my worth. It was rooted in fear of never being good enough. I can see it so plainly now. When the opportunity arose to join a new company that focused on hair care that was labeled the "next best thing," I jumped at it. And almost overnight, it blew up.

Before I knew it, I was having the most success I've ever had. I was on cloud nine. I became obsessed with performing, ranking up, and learning more about this business model. I began reading all the books about success in life and became hooked on personal development. I felt like an adrenaline junkie honestly. Every time someone commented on a post or video online, asking for more information about the company, I would run to my Facebook messenger to sell them some shampoo or see if they wanted to join my team. It was like a shot of dopamine every single time I got a new order. I spent every single lunch hour at my teaching job on my phone, answering messages or talking to my teammates. It seemed like everyone wanted this magical shampoo and after only three months in, I even earned the "free" car from the company! A status symbol that I was very eager to accomplish and brought me the recognition that I was craving.

But... I was also married, remember? That guy I chose to share a life with? I was leaving him in the dust. Instead of focusing on fostering a new marriage, I was more concerned with ranking up in my business. When Cody would ask me for help, it went

10 Things I Hate About My Husband

something like this:

> "Oh, you want me to come help you rope tonight? Sorry, I have a call to get on."
> "Oh, you want me to go check cows with you? Sorry, I can't. I've got way too many messages to get back to."

Still to this day, I get sick to my stomach, thinking of all the times I put my business over my husband. I pretended not to see his shoulders sag when I told him my work was more important than helping him in the roping pen. I puffed out my chest with an "I dare you to challenge me" attitude when he asked me to get off my phone and just be present. If he complained at all about my business taking up too much time, I immediately reminded him of how much money I was making and that my dreams mattered too.

Key word there is "too." You see, for the first few years of our life, between dating, getting engaged, and then getting married, Cody's career came first. Most of our life revolved around roping and rodeo. And a part of me did love it very much. I supported him and wanted him to have success because his dreams became my dreams. I told myself that my business success would help him accomplish those dreams. So, when he challenged me about my business by telling me I was on my phone too much, it was like punching me right in the gut. Didn't he realize that I was doing this for him, too?

In the world of network marketing, you sacrifice now to enjoy the fruits of your labor later. I repeatedly heard phrases like: "Your kid won't even know you missed his baseball game. Make the sacrifice now so you can have the freedom to do anything you want later." So that's what I thought I was doing. Sacrificing now (which meant ignoring my husband), so we could have more money and more freedom later.

Every time Cody asked me to help him or I put my business on hold to support him, resentment started building up. My blood

46

would boil and my heart would race thinking about the messages and the calls and the work I could and should be doing, instead of actually spending time with my husband.

I know now, the devil was planting lies in my head such as *He clearly doesn't care about my dreams because he's annoyed I'm on my phone*; or *He's the self-centered one because I've always supported him and now it's my turn to have success and he hates it*; or *Doesn't he see that I'm doing this for him, too?*

I had created a story of competition between the two of us and had not only this spirit of mammon taking root, but also an idol of success. As always, I had good intentions of what my business was doing. But the devil used those good intentions to create a wedge between Cody and I that said "your dreams don't matter as much as his and there is just no way to be a team now."

This is harder than I imagined admitting to you; but in reality, I know this is so common! The CEO businessman who stays at the office late every night who justifies it as providing for his family. The small business momma who never sleeps and works around the clock because she feels like it is her calling, yet her family desperately needs her. The reality is that it isn't always the man who is caught up in performance and striving; women are just as susceptible.

I will never forget February 2018. I had a choice to make between attending one of my best friend's weddings or going to my company's Leadership Summit that I had qualified for. After seeking advice from my mentors, it was highly recommended that I choose business over the wedding, which is what I did. And as I called my friend, crying my eyes out, to let her know I wouldn't be at her wedding, it was like I lost a little piece of my soul. It was one more sacrifice I was willing to make in the name of success.

On top of that, my grandmother passed away while I was at the convention. I was not there to hold her hand one last time and tell her that I loved her. I was not there to comfort my mom. I was not there to mourn this huge loss in my life. And after my mom called me and told me the news and encouraged me to try and enjoy the party that night at the event, I wiped my tears, put on a happy face and showed up.

I compartmentalized my emotions because that's what big girls do. I plastered a smile on my face during the party and posed for a picture with my pregnant belly. The comments flooded in: "You are so gorgeous." "Look at that bump!" "Congratulations on earning your trip!" And it validated me. It gave me the confirmation that I needed to justify the fact that I was making the right choice to choose business over everything else in my life.

It makes me sad when I think about who I was back then. I was made of stone. I was living on the surface of my life, just doing what I needed to do to keep up. Not feeling my emotions, but just running towards these goals and this future that I desperately thought I needed.

Now, please don't hear me wrong. There is nothing wrong with being ambitious and driven and wanting to provide for your family. I don't think wanting more for your life is a bad thing. I believe 100% that God gives us visions and goals to work towards and I love what Habakkuk 2:2-3 says, "*Then the LORD said to me, 'Write my answer plainly on tablets, so that a runner can carry the correct message to others. This vision is for a future time. It describes the end, and it will be fulfilled. If it seems slow in coming, wait patiently, for it will surely take place. It will not be delayed.*" (NLT)

Having vision is a great thing, but it becomes an issue when it becomes your idol. It becomes an issue when it becomes your identity. And that is what it became for me. An identity. I was finding my worth in success. I was riding the coattails of success like my life depended on it. This version of me that I had become, where I had to hide my emotions, hide my struggles, and sacrifice special moments with my family. It was stripping away my light. It was making me a slave to something that could actually never fulfill me long term.

Shayla Huber

My life changed forever on April 18, 2018, when Leroy Kenneth joined our family. I became a mom for the first time and could not even explain the love that I was feeling for my new baby boy. I was so hopeful that Cody and I would stop fighting so much, because I was hoping I could slow down in my business some. I was determined to find more balance between work and family.

On the outside, it looked like we absolutely had it all together. And I told myself that we had made it. We were able to afford to eat where we wanted to eat. We were able to buy what we wanted to buy. We weren't worried about the cost of diesel or gas. We were on the rodeo road as a family and all my sacrifices had paid off. I told Cody, "See, I told you this business was going to bring us a lot of money. See? I told you this is why I worked so hard. This was the plan all along." I gladly took the credit for all of this "freedom" we were experiencing.

And then 2019 hit. It all happened so fast I didn't even see it coming. My business started going backwards. People were deciding to leave my team, my paycheck was decreasing, customers were canceling and I was having a hard time getting new people started. The company I was partnered with was hit hard with rumors and false accusations and it was out of my control. It was like an absolute night and day difference from enrolling 10-20 people per month personally, to radio silence. Through this fiasco, I was determined to not lose my business. The ship was sinking fast, and I thought it was up to me to keep it afloat.

My breaking point came when I was sitting in front of my computer, with the goal of messaging 20 people, and while holding Leroy in my arms I wept. Tears were streaming down my face. It was the realization that my business wasn't my greatest source of success and joy anymore, but the source of defeat, failure, and pressure.

I was exhausted, but I was willing to try anything different to get away from this pit of despair I found myself in. The pain felt unbearable and the weight of what we would do without me making more money in my business terrified me.

Of course, I did the next logical thing I could think of. I spent thousands of dollars (and I mean thousands) on a mentorship program that promised to teach me how to attract my ideal customers and business partners and make even more money doing it as an affiliate! Without even praying about it or caring about the price tag, I jumped in head first. I was so tired of private messaging people to join me and hearing crickets or rejection.

And while some great things came out of this investment, it was still one more way that I was chasing money, chasing success, and grabbing at anything I could that would help me to feel fulfilled in some way. It was my way of saying "God, I don't need you. I'll figure it out. This has to be what I'm supposed to be doing, right?"

And here is the irony of it all: We didn't have the money to pay for this program, so I went back into debt in order to fund this investment. I felt the promise of this program so strongly, that I figured, if it worked, I would just pay it back off like my other massive loan I had already taken care of. *If I can do it once, I guess I can do it again*, I thought. My supportive husband must have been incredibly confused. One minute I was budgeting every penny and yelling at him about buying a pop at the gas station, and the next I was applying for credit cards to pay for this program. Talk about being double-minded.

However, he trusted me that I was making the best decision for me and so I spent the next year growing and learning in the online marketing space.

Here is the truth about making success your idol. It will never, ever fulfill you. No matter how much money you make or how much recognition you receive from the world—you will still feel empty. Just like Solomon wrote in Ecclesiastes 2:11 *"But as I looked at everything I had worked so hard to accomplish, it was all so meaningless-like chasing the wind. There was nothing really worthwhile anywhere."* (NLT)

That is exactly what it felt like… chasing the wind. I felt miserable and unhappy behind closed doors. And yet on camera, I was the boss babe with the baby on her hip. I was the boss babe talking about making money from home, when my income was tanking and my debts were rising. I masked all of my worries so no one would find out. I held onto the mindset of "when I get to this point with my income, then I'll be happy."

I kept promising Cody. "I just need to get to this level, and then I can slow down. If I just get to this level, then I'll support you more and not be so snappy at you. You aren't the only one pursuing a big dream, remember? My dreams matter, too!" Those superficial and worldly dreams were enough to keep me walking this path of destruction. It was enough for me to keep running ads with money I didn't have (and trying to hide it from Cody). It was enough to keep neglecting my family with work during holidays and special occasions. It was enough for me to keep holding on to the stories in my head about my husband not supporting me, understanding me, or being on the same page with me.

The reason I'm being so open and honest about this season of my life, is because I know how relatable it is. I know some of you have been chasing the wind. That career path that you think will give you the status symbol and recognition you deserve. The money that you think will bring you safety. The designer clothes and car that you believe will make you appear like you have it all together to the other moms in the school pick-up lane. You expect the perfect relationship with your husband or kids because you think if they would just get it together, then you would be happy and life would be easier. You dream of a life with more ease, more perfection, and less chaos—but you are seeking them in circumstances, things and people. You've been longing and probably even praying for a breakthrough in some area of your life but feel no peace about any of it because you haven't "made it yet." Sound familiar?

It wasn't until years later that I realized I was living like an orphan in this world. Even though I believed in God, I didn't know him as my father, or recognize His love for me. I didn't know my identity was as a chosen daughter of God and that I could trust him with everything. My logical brain wanted that—but my heart screamed that I was alone. My heart posture was that of "DO-HAVE-BE."

I have to "do" this thing and perform (work my business) before I can "have" the results (appear successful in that business) and then I can finally "be" that version of myself that I am envisioning (be satisfied and happy with my life). This type of thinking kept me in the cycle of doing more, striving more and hustling more. Whereas what God says is "BE-HAVE-DO." Once you can rest and "be" who God says you are (which is His daughter), you can "have" the peace and joy and freedom he promises, then you can go and "do" the assignment He gives you.

In Psalm 51:16-17 David writes to God: *"You do not desire a sacrifice, or I would offer one. You do not want a burnt offering. The sacrifice you desire is a broken spirit. You will not reject a broken and repentant heart, O God."* (NLT) It's true, we can never please God by our works and our good deeds do not bring us salvation. What God desires is our heart. What he cares about is our lives, trusting and yearning for Him. It's a relationship based on identity, repentance and love. Not hustle, striving or earning.

Sister, the only way to get out of the rat race of chasing success and the things of this world is to know who you are and whose you are. Otherwise, your marriage will continue suffering. Your parenting will continue suffering. And that emptiness will eventually catch up to you until one day, you are on your knees—begging God to take away the pain.

This is where I found myself in January 2020. I was drowning. I was sick of lying to myself that things were going to get better. I was sick of getting my hopes up. I felt tired of pretending that I was happy, when deep down I didn't like who I had become. I came to the realization that I had spent thousands of dollars chasing a dream that wasn't happening. I had quite literally put my family in a financial pickle, chasing a dream I wasn't sure I wanted in the first place anymore. It all seemed futile.

I'll never forget sitting on my couch, reading my Bible and I had the sudden urge to pray on my knees. This is not something that I normally did and it felt super awkward. But I went to my room and kneeled next to my bed and with tears streaming down my face—I asked God for guidance. I begged him for a solution. I cried out in so much pain and frustration to a God that I knew in my head but didn't really know in my heart. And for the first time in a very long time—I heard His voice. He told me to message my friend Sarah. I literally couldn't shake it. I had connected with her the summer before and she had been telling me about a new company she was with and how much she loved it. I hadn't given it too much thought until this very moment. The nudge was so very strong that I remember standing up, walking to my tiny laundry room, and sending her voice message after voice message, crying and asking for help. "I don't really know why I'm reaching out to you, other than God is asking me to. Please tell me about your company. Tell me more."

At one of the lowest points in my life, God met me. He opened my eyes to what I actually needed. Jesus said: "*Look! I stand at the door and knock. If you hear my voice and open the door, I will come in, and we will share a meal together as friends.*" Revelation 3:20 (NLT) Even though I had been walking away from Him, relying on my own strength to solve all my problems, He still turned His face to me. He guided me in the right direction. And I finally decided to listen. I had been orchestrating God in my life at this point and now God was going to start orchestrating mine. This defining moment and eventual business pivot led me to finding my true identity in Christ, as a loved and cherished daughter. Slowly but surely, God was moving me in the right direction.

At the end of the day, worldly pursuits, careers, and idols are a way for Satan to distract and divide us. Marriage is the furthest thing from a competition, it is designed to make you and your husband united. So, any thought you have around your husband being the enemy or competition, is sure to be a lie from Satan. He loves to fill our brains with thoughts of worldly success and accomplishments being more important than our spouse and the snowball effect can have major consequences. He is sneaky, but he isn't really clever. Identity and competition are two areas where he likes to stir up conflict, confusion, and chaos which we will dive deeper into in the upcoming chapters!

SCRIPTURE:

Romans 7:20-25 (NLT)

"But if I do what I don't want to do, I am not really the one doing wrong, it is sin living in me that does it. I have discovered this principle of life-that when I want to do what is right, I inevitably do what is wrong. I love God's law with all my heart. But there is another power within me that is at war with my mind. This power makes me a slave to the sin that is still within me. Oh, what a miserable person I am! Who will free me from this life that is dominated by sin and death? Thank God! The answer is in Jesus Christ our Lord. So you see how it is: In my mind I really want to obey God's law, but because of my sinful nature I am a slave to sin."

PRAYER:

Father, forgive me for any idols I have created in my life. Forgive me for any competition I have created between my spouse in the name of success. Help me to see today that we are one. Help me to see how much you deeply care about both of our lives and are orchestrating all things for good, in your precious son's name. Thank you for being a good and caring Father as I learn more and more about my identity in you. You are patient and kind. Help me to understand how my actions have hurt those in my life. I am ready for a renewed mind and to find my peace in you and you alone. Amen.

QUESTIONS:

1. Identify any idols in your life by finishing this statement: "I can't live without _____." Our priorities should be God, husband, children, job and when we fall out of this order, we tend to get in trouble! Take time to really process your own priorities and how you are showing up in life.

2. What is your view of success? Does it determine your worth? Is it something that you find yourself chasing, whether that be in business, motherhood, or some other area of life? Study James 1:16-18 and ask God what He says about success!

3. Write down BE-HAVE-DO to remind yourself that it isn't what you DO that matters to God, it's who you ARE.

4.
Pick Up Your Dang Clothes

Have you ever said to your husband, "Babe! Would you please pick up your dang clothes?!" in a not so loving tone? Yep, that's what I thought!

There was nothing more annoying to me than Cody coming home, taking off his clothes (clothes that had literal cow poop and mud on them from working cattle that day) and tossing them haphazardly to where they landed half inside the washer or half inside the hamper. Or my personal favorite -- when the socks and t-shirt didn't even make it anywhere near a hamper and they were sprawled out all over the floor. I do not, for the life of me, understand how he missed the concept of where to put dirty clothes. I mean—wouldn't it just take half a second for him to pay attention to where the hamper is? Apparently, that's not worth the effort, and if you're anything like me, this "dirty laundry amnesia" husbands seem to develop is beyond frustrating and sometimes downright hurtful.

I'm talking about dirty towels and clothes left on the bathroom floor after taking his nightly shower or the extra dishes he used that never made it to the sink, and instead, piled up on his nightstand. Now, my husband is not a slob. He takes two showers a day, appreciates a clean house, and if I ask for help, he will help; no questions asked. It just does not come naturally for him to be an active participant in the household or take initiative in certain areas. If your husband sounds a lot like my husband in this respect, then chances are he most likely was raised in a very traditional home, with very traditional values. In the type of home where the husband does all the outside work like mowing the yard, taking out the trash or in my case, feeding the multitude of cows and horses, while the wife does all the inside stuff like cooking, sweeping the floor, and cleaning. Sound familiar? Combine these traditional gender roles with the fact that my mother-in-law also has the nature to do everything for everyone, it's no wonder that my husband expected these things out of me. I can't be mad at the guy for operating the only way he knows how, right?

Wrong. So wrong. Oh, did I ever boil inside sometimes when I felt like I was constantly picking up after Cody. I made little sarcastic comments out of the side of my mouth about it (you know what I'm talking about) and told him that I wasn't his mother. I would nag and complain on repeat to no avail. Afterwards I would have an out-of-body experience, where I could hear myself as the "nagging wife" and it honestly made me sick. I began to feel a lot of shame and guilt around the fact that I could never hold my tongue or that I cared so much about the laundry being on the floor, because, at the end of the day, I cared about being a good wife. I cared about serving my family. I desired to be like my mother-in-law in this area, who spent her days solely focused on her family and home and did it so seamlessly. But all of my multitude of responsibilities were taking its toll on me.

Taking care of my family and home was just one of my jobs. I also had a business I was trying to run. A business, remember, that stressed me out and was something I had a hard time putting down. A business, remember, that held my identity in the palm of its hand, reminding me I was a failure if I wasn't succeeding. *I knew Cody worked incredibly hard during the day, but didn't he see that I was also working hard? Didn't he see me way in over my head, struggling to keep up with the kids, the cooking, the cleaning and my business? How many times did I have to remind him how busy I am?* Those are the thoughts I would have daily. The resentment I was feeling towards him was building and it created a cold and silent atmosphere in our home that I hated. I felt so unloved when my husband didn't see my struggles and didn't feel the need to help me. I felt neglected and unseen. And it wasn't until just a few months ago that God really showed me the deeper reason why I felt this way.

With this bruised heart of mine, I nagged Cody to death and made him feel bad about not doing the little things. I became a martyr, doing all the things for everyone, and not being appreciated for any of it. I would clean up the kitchen and then rudely ask Cody if he noticed. Or I would list off all of the things I accomplished that day with a "beat that!" kind of attitude. I didn't like how it felt, but I couldn't control myself. The rude comments would just fall right out of my mouth, like leaves falling from a tree. I desperately wanted him to acknowledge all of my efforts and tell me he was proud of me. I wanted him to validate that I was doing a good job. And when he wouldn't, I went fishing for it.

When I tried to understand why something as little as not picking up his clothes made me so mad, I couldn't come up with a single good reason. I knew I felt hurt, but I didn't understand the deeper heart wounds that were at work here. And then again, guilt and shame would creep up and whisper in my ear: "You are a terrible wife. Just get over it. You are such an angry person. You shouldn't let such little things get to you."

The lies would suffocate me and I would just shut down. I would go through the motions of picking up the house, but not with an attitude of serving my husband and kids. I felt very sad and mopey, and when Cody would ask what's wrong, my answer was a snappy "nothing." I saw myself as a victim or a doormat. I was always giving and getting nothing in return. Bitterness was rising and I started to fear that I would have to live like this forever and that maybe this is just what marriage is like.

January 2020 became a turning point for me. I made a bold, business pivot that I truly felt God had orchestrated and I joined a new company and team and was determined to have a different experience. I wanted to approach building a business in a new way—without the hustle and the striving that I was used to. At the time, I wasn't sure how to make that happen, but I knew I had found the right mentorship that would guide me in the right direction. I was tired of chasing success for all the wrong reasons. I was burnt-out, stressed out, and completely out of alignment with my life and beyond ready for a change. The Mental Wellness Company seemed like the perfect pivot to make in my life, with products that would help my mental wellness, gut health, and physical health.

Within the first three months, I started noticing such a huge difference in my physical and mental health. I started sleeping better and having more energy during the day. My bloating after eating went away and I no longer had frequent stomach aches. My tension headaches that I had chalked up to being a "boss mom" started disappearing, and I was noticing that I had more patience and presence with my son. I went from parenting on the couch to playing on the floor with him. We started going on little day trips and having dance parties in the kitchen. I was feeling so much better in so many ways!

This shift in my health also impacted my relationship with Cody. For once, I didn't care about the clothes not being in the hamper. I actually had more energy to tidy up the house and more motivation to clean. My anxiety and sadness were replaced with happiness and joy. Instead of dreading each day, I felt excited for what each day would bring.

Suddenly, my husband's neglect of his clothes didn't make me want to crawl out of my skin anymore. I found myself with stress resilience for the first time ever. What exactly is stress resilience? The American Psychological Institute defines resilience as, "the process of adapting well in the face of adversity, trauma, tragedy, threats, or significant sources of stress." Keywords here are "adapting well."

I was not usually a go with the flow type of person—quite the opposite. I liked having a plan and when the plan would get off course, I felt like a rug was pulled out from under me. Which in our life, was pretty much every day! Stress resilience not only helps in the really big moments in life, like handling a big move, job change, or unexpected loss of a loved one… but it also matters in the small, mundane moments too. And as a mom, this was a game changer. I was able to go from doing laundry to doing the dishes to handling a toddler tantrum with ease and energy. I could record a video for my business with Leroy on my hip without getting totally distracted and thrown off by his smiles and giggles. I felt like the supermom version of the energizer bunny. The brain fog that had hindered my ability to focus and be present had lifted, and I was becoming a more care-free version of myself. A much better version of myself.

I remember a specific situation where I was changing Leroy's diaper in the living room. He was at the stage where changing his diaper was the last thing he wanted to do. He would either kick his legs and laugh, or he would kick his legs and cry. Anything he could think of to get out of changing his poopy butt. Boys are so gross. But anyways, I used to get so angry at this. It seems like such a small task, but it was something that would stress me out and I would have little patience for it. But on this particular day, I can remember being more prepared. I laid Leroy out on the floor. Got the diaper and wipes ready and proceeded to change his diaper. And when the legs went to kickin'… I went to ticklin'! I started tickling his belly. I started singing to him. I started to do anything I could to distract him, and it worked! He was laughing and smiling and gave me a big hug when we got his new diaper on.

That was not the version of myself that I had known, but it was a version that I liked very much. And feeling like a gentle, loving, and patient mom in that moment brought me to tears. I never wanted to be the yelling mom or the nagging wife. I wanted to find joy in the little things, and it felt like that was finally happening. It was like I was a butterfly emerging from my cocoon that had suffocated me for way too long.

As I started to grow this new business, my mentor started coaching me on things that I had never considered before. Things like how your health and how you fuel your body does make a difference in your business results and in your overall mood. The bottom line is, when you feel better, you do better. When you have more energy and motivation, you will do the actions necessary to build your business. When you aren't crabby and exhausted, you show up differently in your home! When you are giving a little more care to yourself, you can give more care to others.

This is exactly what was happening, and it was revolutionary in my life and marriage. As a result of these small changes I was making, Cody and I started connecting again. I was less focused on what he wasn't doing for me and more focused on taking care of my mind, body, and soul. My husband and circumstances were not the things that changed. It was me that was changing. I took the finger that I had pointed at him for so long— and I began to point it at myself. Not in condemnation or shame, but in love and in a desire to do better for the people around me.

Now, this might sound like a very surface level answer to the original problem of "I don't feel loved because my husband never helps me out." I would totally agree. That is not something that you can just ignore long term. But at the time, I had no idea the heart wounds I had been holding on to from my past. I didn't fully understand why his dirty laundry on the floor literally felt like a slap on the cheek. I had no idea that the attention and the love and the validation I so desperately wanted from my husband were rooted in a past with divorced parents and a dad who I missed with my whole heart. I had no idea that I was projecting those heart wounds onto my husband and truly believed that he was the answer to all of my problems. But focusing on my mental and physical health—it was a great first step. It was peeling back the first layer of a wounded heart that would eventually lead to even more self-awareness and understanding.

I want to encourage you to think about the steps you can take to start peeling back the layers of your own heart. Maybe like me, you can start with your health. Ask yourself these questions:

- How are you treating your body?
- What is your diet like?
- What type of foods are you eating?
- Are you moving your body at all?
- Are you making any form of exercise a priority?
- What is the status of your mental health?
- Do you find yourself easily stressed and anxious?
- Do you feel unhappy and sad most of the time?

You may have told yourself that you're just going to feel bad the rest of your life, so you better get used to it. You may be used to living with headaches, bloating, and mood swings, but it isn't normal or healthy. Feeling like you are running on an empty tank does not have to be your reality anymore. One of the first steps you can take is to optimize your gut brain connection by focusing on sleep, a clean diet, and moving your body. Just by making these small changes in your daily life you can significantly improve your mental health, which is the start to a happier and healthier you.

After all, our bodies are God's temple. 1st Corinthians 6:19-20 says: *"Don't you realize that your body is the temple of the Holy Spirit, who lives in you and was given to you by God? You do not belong to yourself, for God bought you with a high price. So you must honor God with your body."* (NLT) Now, this does not mean to make your health an idol or an obsession. We don't need to go to any extremes here. But we can become more self-aware of what our bodies need to function better. We can learn more about the natural ways that God designed our bodies to thrive in order to actually enjoy our lives here on earth. Why would He want us feeling blah and unmotivated? Why would He want us feeling sick and struggling with the day to day of our lives? Well, the answer is that He doesn't! That's a breeding ground for the enemy to come in to fill our heads with lies around being stuck, unhappy, and not able to live into our full potential. God wants us living, breathing, and moving as vibrant and healthy sons and daughters!

10 Things I Hate About My Husband

Many of us women struggle with low self-image and low self-worth. Which again, tells us that it's a waste of time to pour into ourselves and what is the point? But what does God say about our worth? We are not worthy because of anything we do, but because of Jesus. He sent Jesus to die on the cross for our sins, to save us from our sinful nature, and bring us eternal life. As a result, we are adopted into His royal family. The fact that God did that for us is the ultimate loving sacrifice. And when we struggle with low self-worth, it means we are not receiving the precious gift that we have been given. This keeps us separated from our loving Father and the fully alive life that He wants us to have! When you can start to see yourself as God sees you everything changes.

That year, I gave myself permission to take care of myself. I started to see it as "me too." I can take care of my family, but I need to take care of myself too. When I take care of myself, I can show up and be the wife and mom that God has called me to be. When the brain fog lifted, I saw everything in a brand-new light, completely opposite of how I had been before. I went from a "hustle, push through, sacrifice myself" approach, to a rest and nurture approach.

When I started this journey of self-discovery, I realized how much coasting I had done up until then. I had been just going through the motions, and not really understanding why I did any of the things that I did. I was always reacting to things instead of stopping to respond. For example, when I was stressed, I would reach for a chocolate bar instead of asking myself a question about what is causing the stress and what would be a better option here? Or when my son would throw a tantrum, I would yell or discipline him instead of reminding myself that this is a developmental milestone he is going through and what response would be better for him?

I had let my feelings and emotions control my life and had justified it by believing that it was just my personality. I just love chocolate. I'm just a yelling mom. This is just "who I am." But as my eyes were opened and I was surrounded by other women who were on very similar journeys—I was starting to understand all the lies I had believed about myself up until that point, and how the devil liked to use shame and guilt to keep me spiraling out of control. I was starting to understand I had more control over my life than I had given myself credit for and that change can be a very, very good thing.

As a result of this newfound awareness and understanding, I became hungry for growth. Not outward growth in terms of business numbers and enrollments, but personal growth that was internal and deep. I wanted my outside circumstances to reflect how I was actually feeling on the inside. No more faking it until I make it. No more painting a picture on social media of sunshine and rainbows, while I was internally sopping wet from the rain. I wanted to live with integrity, honor and grace for myself. I realized in order to achieve business results, you must also focus on other areas of your life because they are all interconnected. Your health, relationships, mindset, faith… it's all connected and they all matter. They have the power to impact each other in many different ways.

I'll never forget one of the most important conversations I had with my mentor, Cassie, in those first few months of being part of this new company. I had some serious momentum when it came to this personal growth stuff and I was clearly hooked. I was on every team call, with my notebook and pen, taking notes and implementing what I was learning. I was journaling and reading books and discovering so much about myself. But there was one thing I was still very much hung up on --my marriage.

I absolutely loved the growth I was experiencing internally, but my husband wanted no part of it. I was scaling a mountain and he wasn't coming with me. I felt so annoyed that while I seemed to be running fast towards this better life—he was firmly planted in his old ways. No amount of convincing would get him to pick up a book or listen to a podcast with me and the gap between us seemed to be rising again.

10 Things I Hate About My Husband

I had taken one big leap forward in helping our marriage by taking care of my health only for us to take two steps back because we weren't on the same personal growth journey. While on the phone with Cassie one day, I said with frustration in my voice, "He just doesn't get it! Why won't he listen to me? Sometimes it feels like we are growing apart even more and fighting about all of the ways we are different. I just wish he would understand." And with compassion and love in her voice, she explained that people grow at different speeds. We don't need to force them into our box, meaning it's ok to love someone where they are at, while you continue to grow.

For whatever reason, her response really hit me hard. Hearing her say those words helped me to release control of trying to change my husband, while giving myself permission to keep growing personally. Even though it felt like it at the time, our marriage wasn't falling apart just because we weren't totally on the same page. But in my quest for my own growth, I had inadvertently pushed my marriage aside.

It was obvious that if I needed to hone in on any area of my life at this point in time, it was my marriage. And so that's what I did. I decided right then and there that I was going to learn more about my role in our marriage and how to take some responsibility in how I was responding to him. Maybe it wasn't that he was such a horrible human being; maybe I just needed to understand myself and marriage more. There is so much more to unpack here, and I promise we will!

I want to stress to you that you are in control of your feelings and emotions. You don't have to feel shame and guilt around how you've responded to your husband in the past. You can move from reactive mode, to respond mode as you get to know yourself better. You can move from being the nagging wife we see in Proverbs 25:24 to the Proverbs 31 wife, who is clothed with strength and dignity. Just as Paul says in 2 Corinthians 10:5 to take our thoughts captive and make them obedient to Christ, you can make a decision today to grab a hold of your internal life. To stop assuming the worst about your husband and all the ways he is lacking, and instead focus on your own growth. You can take a step today, to decide to give yourself some attention. I mean, reading this book alone shows you take initiative to better yourself! I'm so proud of you!

Let's set one goal right now to move you in the right direction. Remember, focusing on my mental and physical health was a great starting point for me that helped my mood, anxiety, energy, gut health and overall outlook on life. It gave me clarity of mind and motivation to do the little tasks around the house that used to be daunting and annoying, like picking up those dang clothes on the ground. You don't need to do a complete overhaul of your entire life (that actually will do more harm than good), but you can start small and just choose one habit that can make a big difference long term. It can be ordering supplements (see my QR code at the back of this book for more information) and consistently taking them. It can be committing to a new gym and weightlifting program. It can be upping your water intake or cutting out one sugary food or drink that always gives you a terrible crash later. There are truly so many different options!

Whatever you decide to do, my prayer is that you do it consistently and are able to experience how showing up better for yourself positively affects how you show up for others. Don't be afraid to start small. Just start! Your mental health (and your husband) will thank you later!

SCRIPTURE:
Romans 12:1-2 (NLT)
"And so, dear brothers and sisters, I plead with you to give your bodies to God because of all he has done for you. Let them be a living and holy sacrifice- the kind he will find acceptable. This is truly the way to worship him. Don't copy the behavior and customs

of this world, but let God transform you into a new person by changing the way you think. Then you will learn to know God's will for you, which is good and pleasing and perfect."

PRAYER:

Father God, thank you for creating me the way that you have. As Jeremiah 29 says, I know the plans you have for me are to thrive in this life, in body, mind and spirit. Forgive me for any neglect or abuse that I have given my body and my spouse and help me to see my true worth in you. Help me to see that I am worthy of being a vibrant and present wife, who understands and takes care of herself. I know that having a healthy marriage with my husband is one of your great gifts and I take responsibility for the part I play in that. I'm ready and eager to transform my body, mind and soul to fulfill your mighty plans in my life. Amen.

QUESTIONS:

1. What goal are you setting today to work towards better mental and/or physical health?
2. Write down some of the emotions you feel when your husband does not help around the house. We will be coming back to this question later.
3. Visualize what life will be like if you felt better, had more energy, and genuinely looked forward to your days?

5.
Complete Opposites

Time for some Sunday School 101! I promise you'll see the point I'm making in a little bit.

Genesis 1:7 *"Then the LORD God formed the man from the dust of the ground. He breathed the breath of life into the man's nostrils, and the man became a living person."*

Genesis 1:27 *"So God created human beings in his own image. In the image of God he created them; male and female he created them."*

Genesis 2:23-24 *"At last!" the man exclaimed. "This one is bone from my bone, and flesh from my flesh! She will be called 'woman,' because she was taken from 'man.'"* This explains why a man leaves his father and mother and is joined to his wife, and the two are united into one.

As we can see from Scripture, from the beginning men and women were created differently. The man was made from dust and the woman was made from the man's ribs. And yet, they were both made in the image of God and they were created to perfectly complement each other. I want you to hold tight to that imagery during this chapter.

I was raised in the church. I was raised to know who my Creator is and how God created all of humankind. I know the story of Adam and Eve like the back of my hand, just like you probably do if you were raised in church too. But knowing how God created Eve from Adam did nothing to prepare me for living with a man. Especially a man who has very little in common with me. Gah!

I'm not sure if you had a similar experience or not, but I

10 Things I Hate About My Husband

didn't care when we were dating that my husband wasn't a reader like me. I didn't care that he hated school and I loved school. I didn't care that I preferred 90's country music and he liked more of the Texas red dirt tunes. I simply didn't pay attention to our differences because I was head over heels in love. We can figure our differences out later!

And boy did we ever. The ways in which we were opposite soon became glaringly clear. I need a solid eight hours of sleep to function properly. Cody seems to get along just fine with three after pulling an all-nighter on the rodeo road. I love to talk about my hopes and dreams and Cody likes to live in the now. I am full of words (seriously I can talk for hours) and Cody is a man of few words. I like to save my money; Cody tends to spend it. I'm the planner, Cody goes with the flow. I prefer texting or sending voice notes and Cody prefers calling you on the phone, like we still live in the 90's or something. I love trying new food and will eat just about anything, but Cody wants to eat steak and potatoes for every meal! Every single meal. Please tell me I'm not the only one!

These differences began to create so much intensity and frustration in our marriage because I just wanted to feel like we had something in common—more like sunshine and rainbows, less like cats and dogs! One of my biggest desires was to feel like I had a teammate in my husband. That we could work together, pray together, and grow together. And at this time in our marriage, we were so far from that ideal that it felt like it would never come to pass. When we were stuck in the truck driving somewhere, I saw it as an opportunity to talk. And not just talk about ordinary things, but deep talks about our future children, our dream house, and our passions and callings in life. Talks about God and the deeper meaning of life and who we are supposed to be.

Cody, however, did not share my same desire for soul-baring conversation. He preferred to listen to music or turn on a show or do literally anything else besides talking about dreams. I knew he had a beautiful soul inside his chest. I knew he had his

70

own hopes and dreams. But for some reason, he preferred to keep them in his own heart and mind and I felt desperate to get them out of him. Like I wanted to free a caged bird.

As I mentioned in the previous chapter, my focus on personal growth and development seemed to be widening this gap between us. I would read something in a book and have an aha moment and really want Cody to read it too, and he would say "no thanks." He didn't need to read or listen to podcasts. He didn't see the need to grow in his mental game or in his faith. The practice pen was enough for him, but it wasn't for me. I didn't understand why he was discrediting other resources that were there to help someone like him become better. To find success and fulfillment and purpose. I truly, from the bottom of my heart, just wanted to help him. Instead of backing off when he shrugged off my suggestions, I pushed harder. "Seriously babe, read this! I think you will love it!" I was on a mission to become the best version of myself for me and my family and wanted to bring Cody along for the ride.

When it became obvious he didn't share the same idea—it hurt. I took it as him not wanting to be his best self. Which I internalized as he must not care that much about us, because if he did he would want to be better for me and our boys. If the changes I was making were helping those around me, why couldn't my husband do the same thing?

The more I pushed, the worse I made him feel. I could see him retreating even more into himself. I felt the pain in his words when he told me he was going to be home late again, and I wondered if it was because he really was busy, or he just simply couldn't stand to be around me. I could see the exasperation in his face when he would say, "Nothing is ever good enough for you. Why is that?" I truly thought that I had all the answers and that my way was the right way. His opinions always came second to mine. But actions speak louder than words. It wasn't until I shut my mouth and just stopped pushing that things started to change.

10 Things I Hate About My Husband

I will never forget an experience I had at the beginning of 2021. I had been in this new season of growth for about a year now and was ready to keep going deeper. My business was doing well, but I was ready to take it up a notch. I had recently bought a membership program (much cheaper than the other one I told you about) that was focused on Kingdom business. How to bring God into everything you do. I was learning new strategies when it came to building an online business, and I was loving it. One of the components to this program was heart healing. If you truly desire elevating your business to the next level, allowing God to open up what is in your heart is the place to start. I had done so much mindset work up until this point, that this felt like a great next step. And it was—but not the way I imagined it to be.

I booked the Inner Healing Session, which was an online meeting with a certified facilitator who would pray with me and help me talk with God. This was a completely new experience for me, and even though I was a Christian, hearing from God was something I thought was reserved for the "super" Christians. For the uber faithful ones, like the missionaries and pastors. I wasn't quite as special as them, if you will. So, I was very eager to find out what this inner healing session would entail. I expected God to download some supernatural strategy to me. Or to show me a financial blessing or promise. I just knew that He would reveal something that would 10X my business. But none of those things happened.

As I started praying with my new sister in Christ, she asked me a question I was not prepared for. She asked me where I felt happiest. "What is the very first thing that comes to your mind?" she asked.

And completely caught off guard, I said, "Helping my husband rope." (Which is something I had been doing very little of at this point).

She said, "Okay, tell me more. Where are you and where is your husband?"

As I visualized, I said that I was helping him open the calf chute and he was in the box. It just felt so peaceful. And then she asked me if Jesus was there. And slowly, but surely, Jesus showed up onto the scene. The vision became clearer and clearer and Jesus went from sitting in a chair watching us to coming up to me and putting his arm around me.

I was then asked, "Is there something that Jesus wants you to know right now?"

And as I felt myself come completely undone, I heard Jesus say, "You and Cody are a team."

I could not stop the tears from flowing. I thought this meeting was going to be about my business, but God had other plans. He revealed to me my deepest desire of becoming a team with my husband and gave me the promise that it is already done. He gave me a look into our past and how it was still our future. On the outside, everything seemed fine and dandy. But on the inside, I was filled with fear that Cody and I were not a team. God had seen into my heart the entire time, and here He was, reassuring me that that's the kind of marriage we will have. In that moment, he single-handedly tore down one of the biggest lies I was believing about myself and my marriage.

This experience breathed life into my marriage. It gave me the peace of mind that I didn't need to worry so much about our differences. I just needed to stay focused on God's promises and what I could control in our marriage. Which was ultimately me.

The inner healing session and my conversation with my mentor both helped me to move from wanting my husband to be more like me, and instead choose to focus on my own growth. I was able to accept that people grow differently. Which doesn't mean our marriage is bad, or that we were doing anything wrong. It just means our growth is in a different season from each other, and that's okay. We are allowed to be seasonal.

1 Corinthians 13:4-7 says: *"Love is patient and kind. Love is not jealous or boastful or proud or rude. It does not demand its*

own way. It is not irritable, and it keeps no record of being wronged. It does not rejoice about injustice but rejoices whenever the truth wins out. Love never gives up, never loses faith, is always hopeful, and endures through every circumstance." (NLT)

Now doesn't this sound like two people who are completely opposite of each other simply choosing to love each other? This is one of the most common scriptures read at weddings, and yet when push comes to shove and real marriage hits, it flies right out the window. These verses describe how God loves, and the more we become like Christ through resting in His love for us, the more we can love our spouse. The more we can choose to accept them right where they are and not let our selfish nature win.

Instead of focusing on all the negative ways we were different, I started to study and read books about why we were different. Mainly, he's a man and I'm a woman. Ha! But seriously, we are equals here on planet earth, open to all kinds of opportunities and created for unique purposes. But we most definitely are created differently. God created our innermost beings and needs to be different, and when you start to understand this, you will gain a whole new appreciation for how you and your husband are wired.

For example, as a woman, I am emotional. I want to talk about deep things. I tend to take things personally and hold on to them until we talk about it. When Cody and I have a disagreement, I want to know the why and how to fix it at once so that we can move on and I can understand why Cody was mad in the first place. Cody on the other hand, likes to process on his own and is the opposite of emotional. In fact, my tears literally make him uncomfortable, because cowboys don't cry. He is wired like a manly man and it truly is one of the things I appreciate most about him. But I would like to see some emotion out of him every now and then too, you know what I mean? Is that too much to ask?

My friend Caitlin, and the author of *7 Days to a Life of Limitless*, describes it perfectly. When you think about how men and women are wired, you think of men as having more physical strength than women. There is no denying that my husband can lift hay bales a lot easier than I can. When I need help carrying bags in from the grocery store, Cody can handle more every time. But when it comes to emotional maturity, women have the upper hand. Women know how to explain and communicate their feelings verbally and we generally seek out ways to do just that.

Tension surfaces because we want to emotionally connect with our husbands, but they tend to have a hard time with it. For example, they may have been raised to be a man and men don't cry. They don't sit around campfires talking about their feelings. They just don't. But here is where it gets sticky and where us women need to take a good hard look at how we treat our husbands. Men very rarely make us feel bad for not having the physical strength as they do. They are more than happy to open the pickle jar or chop the firewood needed for winter. But why is it that we are a lot quicker to get upset and point fingers at the fact that our husband isn't emotionally opening up to us?

Not only that, but then we start to think there is something wrong with him or we create a story in our head about them not loving us. (Ask me how I know)! The fact of the matter is, sometimes, they just truly don't know how. They haven't matured emotionally or they simply haven't learned what that looks like in a marriage. Our role is to be their helper; to patiently show them how. Genesis 2:18 says: *"Then the LORD God said, 'It is not good for the man to be alone. I will make a helper who is just right for him.'"* (NLT) In Psalm 124:8 God Himself is referred to as our helper. So, if we were made in the image of God and we were made to be a helper, while it may take some adjusting on our part, this is the role we were created to fulfill.

For many of us, this idea requires a perspective shift. Instead of seeing everything from our angle, we take the time to see our husband's point of view as well. This is incredibly humbling and may take some practice! In my case, when I bring up in conversation something like my thoughts on parenting, or a Bible verse that hit me in all of the right places, or a video I watched that I really resonated with, I have learned that Cody may not respond right away. And he might not ever respond, truthfully. But he listens—and that's a good thing. He may think about it and process it when he is alone.

My job was to invite him into the conversation. I'm sharing my feelings with him, without pushing my agenda on him or expecting anything in return. Now that I understand this is not a strength of his, I don't take it so personally. As the saying goes, you can lead a horse to water, but you can't make him drink. The same goes with our husbands. We can't force them into our way of thinking or magically make them more emotionally mature.

Yes, in some ways it would be great to be able to mold our husbands into the perfect man we wanted him to be, but it's just not realistic or beneficial for us in the long run. I know you may be thinking that this isn't fair or that your needs aren't being met and you wanted me to tell you what to do to get him to see your side. And here I am saying the opposite, tell you to do nothing. I get that and it's understandable. But what God has taught me is that these are the needs that He can meet for me.

These are the times that I run to Him to be filled up with His love so that I have the strength, and patience, and grace to be the Godly wife that I'm called to be. This is the direct invitation and promise that we receive from God. That I can trust Him with my husband and that through my prayers, He is working on maturing and growing Cody into who I need him to be and who God has called him to be.

And on top of how we are wired emotionally, our needs are different too. You might not know this, but a woman has an internal need to be taken care of, while a man has an internal need to be the leader and provider. No wonder most of our fights were around money, business, success, etc. because these internal needs we both had were being challenged and we didn't even know it!

The increased income I made in my business was a direct result of the leadership role I took on and it carried over into my marriage. I knew what I was doing, so Cody should probably listen to me if he wanted to experience more success too. But my constant pushing only made him feel like less of a provider. My constant pushing made me feel like I was not being taken care of and I was carrying the weight of the world on my shoulders.

Ephesians 5:22-26 breaks it down beautifully: *"For wives, this means submit to your husbands as to the Lord. For a husband is the head of his wife as Christ is the head of the church. He is the Savior of his body, the church. As the church submits to Christ, so you wives should submit to your husbands in everything. For husbands, this means love your wives, just as Christ loved the church. He gave up his life for her to make her holy and clean, washed by the cleansing of God's word."* (NLT)

I know what you are thinking. *How do I submit to my husband when he isn't the spiritual leader? When he isn't providing in all of the ways that I need him to? If he ain't fulfilling his part of the bargain, I don't have to do my part either, right?!* These thoughts are exactly what got me into so much trouble and hurt my marriage tremendously, and I don't want that for you. In Chapter 10 I'm going to be doing a deep dive into this conversation when it feels like your husband truly just "doesn't get it!"

Once I understood that my husband has an internal need from God to be the leader and provider of our family, I took a step back. I decided to trust God with my husband and instead of using my demanding words, I started praying over my husband. I prayed over his opportunities and connections. I prayed for his heart. I prayed that I would continue to see him the way that God sees him, as a chosen and loved son. I prayed that his desire to know the Lord would increase, and He would give him guidance to lead our family well.

Ladies, as hard as it might seem sometimes, we must let our husbands lead and we must let God take care of it. Some of us have Type A, controlling personalities that need to take a back seat when it comes to our marriage because our husbands are absolutely capable and willing, but we don't know that because we've never let them take the reins.

Like when we ask him to do the dishes, but we barge in because he isn't doing it right. Or how we ask him to get up with a sick kid in the middle of the night, but he can't seem to get the situation under control, so you bust in there to save the night (angrily I might add). Every time we create space in our life to give our husbands more control, we interrupt them because they aren't doing it "our way," we are not giving them opportunities to be the head of the household. It's bruising their ego and again, taking that internal need away from them. Why would they stick their neck out or give opinions or take control, when we are the ones telling them that their way is the wrong way? They will simply stop trying. Making you more upset because you don't feel taken care of. Is this making sense to you?

Remember when I said that it's time to take radical responsibility for your part of the marriage? This is it. It is time. I promise, when you give him more leading power, he will show up (despite things not being perfect) and he too will be fulfilling his innate desire to lead. You can't pour from an empty cup; neither can your husband. Loving your husband and drawing him closer to God and his God-given nature is one way to help fill his cup.

Let me give you a great example of this. Recently, in the process of remodeling my husband's grandparents' home, I let Cody take the lead. I told him I had way too much I was managing already. My business goals and weekly call schedule, the kids doctor appointments (one was having tonsil surgery and the other having tubes put in), the day to day stuff of cooking, cleaning and decluttering/packing up the house. I was to the point that if I had to take on one more thing mentally, I might completely lose it.

I told him that I needed him to make decisions with the house because I just didn't have the mental capacity to do it.

(Quick note here: It is ok and healthy to ask your husbands to lead and to communicate your needs. They aren't mind readers, remember!) As I stepped down in this area, Cody stepped up! He communicated with our contractor and helped do a lot of the manual labor. He ran back and forth to Menards constantly buying totes, wood, lights and tools. He communicated with the appraiser, the realtor, the electrician, and anyone else we needed help from. And when he needed my help or asked for my opinion, I gave it to him and we made decisions together! It felt amazing to be working as a team and it was actually easier than I had expected.

Prior to this situation, I had been working on releasing control. This seemed to be the final test; what it truly feels like to take a step back and let your husband lead. Through this "test," I believe God was teaching me how to submit to Cody (and teaching me who is ultimately in control, which is God) and he was teaching Cody how to make decisions for our family. It truly was a beautiful experience.

Even though most people say building or remodeling a home and moving is one of the top stressors in life, it went surprisingly well for us. It felt easy. I think a big reason for that is because I let Cody lead and at the same time, my needs were being met too. I felt taken care of. He was providing for our family in a way that I appreciated so much because it was taking something off of my plate. I truly felt so loved throughout the process and I continued to encourage and show my appreciation to him. Something in our spirits shifted when we were in these roles, just as Ephesians 5 describes to us. And as we moved into our newly remodeled home, and I became even more aware of how this experience blessed us, we continued to grow closer together and closer to God.

Being opposite from your husband truly does not have to be a thorn in your side anymore. It does not have to be a lie that you continue to believe any longer. When God said that you are a team, he meant it. *"Two people are better off than one, for they can help each other succeed. If one person falls, the other can reach out and help. But someone who falls alone is in real trouble. Likewise, two people lying close together can keep each other warm. But how can one be warm alone? A person standing alone can be attacked and defeated, but two can stand back to back and conquer. Three are even better, for a triple-braided cord is not easily broken.*" (Ecclesiastes 4:9-12 NLT) God is the third person in our marriage. And with Him at the forefront, teaching us about our roles, pouring out His love on us, and protecting us from the lies of the enemy—we will not break.

As we remember that our husbands are wired differently and have different needs, we can begin to change our perspective. Talk to God about finding opportunities to let your husband lead and start focusing on the good in these differences between men and women. I promise you will start to see your husband in a new way. God was very intentional when he made man and when he made woman. God didn't make a mistake when he created marriage or the roles He designed for us. Even if you don't fit the mold perfectly, I am almost certain you feel these needs in one way or another.

Remember, it is not your job to make your husband more like you. It is not your job to change him or push him into a new version of himself. Romans 12:6 reminds us that "*In his grace, God has given us different gifts for doing certain things well.*" Start exploring you and your husband's gifts and appreciate the differences! Did Jesus push people when he was sharing the gospel? Or did he gently teach and let his actions speak for themselves? Was it a condescending tone to bring people to Christ or was it a genuine and loving nature that brought people to their knees in repentance? His heart was what changed the world and your heart is what can change your home. When God got a hold of me and I started to operate from God's love and my heart wounds began to mend, Cody noticed. And there was a lot more peace in our home.

Once you begin to notice and appreciate your husband's different needs, you might also notice something about how he prefers to show and accept love. Yup, not only are our needs different, but how we experience love is different. Learning how to speak your husband's love language is crucial for a healthy and fulfilling marriage!

NOTE: This chapter can be very sensitive and actually harmful to women in abusive relationships. I am not talking about letting a man lead in the form of abuse or controlling behavior. This is not about allowing toxic behavior to continue. **If you are in a dangerous situation and need help, please seek help! The National Domestic Violence Hotline is 800-799-7233 or seek local help at your church or community centers.** A woman's emotional, spiritual, and physical health come before the institution of marriage and enabling wicked or evil behavior to continue is not at all God's heart. If you are curious if you fall into this category, I recommend the ministry of Leslie Vernick (www.leslievernick.com). You are loved and God wants you safe!

NOTE: Two additional books I recommend diving deeper into the topic of differences between men and women are "Loving Him Well: Practical Advice on Influencing your Husband" By Gary Thomas and "Sex Begins in the Kitchen" by Dr. Kevin Lehman. Check out the references at the back of this book for more information.

SCRIPTURE:
Ephesians 5:1-2 (NLT)
"Imitate God, therefore, in everything you do, because you are his dear children. Live a life filled with love, following the example of Christ. He loved us and offered himself as a sacrifice for us, a pleasing aroma to God."

10 Things I Hate About My Husband

PRAYER:

Father, thank you for the unique and wonderful ways that you made man and woman. It is so amazing and wonderful how you designed marriage to be. Help me to be the wife you created me to be by letting my husband lead. Help me to see all the awesome qualities you gave him. Continue to show Him your love and guide him to be all that you created him to be. Thank you for making us a team and for the ability to grow separately and as one. Amen.

QUESTIONS:

1. Write out your own strengths and write out your husband's. What are the qualities that you love about your husband and how can you show gratitude for them?
2. Where is an area of your life that you could hand over to your husband? This may require you to ask for help and that is ok. Give him an opportunity to show up and be filled up!
3. Dig in deeper if you struggle with control. Ask God to show you the root of it and how to release it to Him. Study Isaiah 55:8-13 and be reminded of God's power, love, and control over all things!

6.
Love Languages

Is it just me, or did you also think that when you got married, your husband would automatically know how to love you? That he would know that you love being told things like "you're beautiful" and "I appreciate you so much?" That he would know that giving you a big hug everyday and a kiss on the forehead would make your knees buckle and make you swoon? That he would know taking out the trash and helping with the dishes without being told would make you so happy you wouldn't be able to wipe the smile off your face?

These things seemed totally obvious to me and the first few years of our marriage, I was so confused by the fact that Cody didn't understand how to love me. I was so irritated that the more he didn't do the things mentioned above, the more unloved I felt.

And as we will uncover in the pages of this chapter are two very important truths. The first being that when we are focused on what we can get out of the marriage, we wind up disappointed. When we have the mindset of "what's in it for me," we miss the beautiful, sacrificial love that God calls us to have for our husband. The type of love that ultimately leads us to His everlasting love. And second, the more we start to understand the love languages and what makes the both of us tick, the more we can love our spouse in a way that makes sense to them, and at best, receive their love in return.

Who knew there was so much to learn about love? Ahh, but it's true what they say, you don't know what you don't know. I assumed that love was love. When you love someone, you do nice things for them, like do the dishes and the laundry. You tell them how much you love them. You give them hugs and hold hands and watch romantic movies together. I mean, that's what I call love! Each day I was showing my love to Cody in these ways but wasn't feeling appreciated because he didn't act like he even cared. I wasn't getting any thank-you's for making suppers or doing anything else in the house. *What in the actual heck? Doesn't he see how hard I am working for him? Why can't he acknowledge me or help out once in a while? This feels like a one-sided relationship and I do not feel loved at all.*

I wish I could say that I kept those thoughts in check and I didn't let the bitterness monster take over me, but boy did I ever unleash my frustration on Cody. I didn't hold back with my words and spoke my mind—complete with screaming, crying and stomping my feet. (Just picture a 3-year old not getting the popsicle she wants and that was basically me.)

I would say things like, "You don't appreciate me. I do all of this for you and you don't do anything for me." My love tank was extremely empty, but here's the kicker—so was his. I was showing him love in all of the ways that I receive love, and he was showing me love in the ways that he receives love. Things like buying me a gift or wanting to spend time with me. He thought that those were the things that would make me giddy with joy, but they were hardly ringing my love bell. So, here we were, both thinking that we were showing each other love, but we were missing the mark. It was a classic case of not speaking each other's love language and on top of that, being hyper-focused on our own needs over the needs of each other.

It pains me to remember the phrase that he would say to me every single time we would have a fight, "I can't do anything right for you," as he would walk away from me, defeated, confused, and upset. We knew we loved each other, but I can remember both of us being so frustrated with the other and not understanding why it was so hard. When it came to expressing our love for each other— we were on two different pages.

When Cody asked me to come help him rope or even just watch him rope, it felt more like a chore than something I wanted to do. He would ask me to go check cows or go somewhere with him, and I just felt like it was kind of a waste of time. I had way too much to do and get done. I would cross my arms, roll my eyes, and say, "I'm too busy." I would think, *I'm not going to give him what he wants, because I'm not getting what I want.* I guess I had no idea what unconditional love was at this point? Yikes. But what I was doing was taking from his love tank because one of the ways he feels love is quality time. By constantly telling him "no, I don't have time for you," he was feeling just as depleted as I was.

Here is another example of this debacle straight from the bedroom. I felt like sex and spending time under the sheets were the only things he wanted to do, and that made me feel used, especially if I wasn't "in the mood." I either would do it to get it over with or say no, and both options left him feeling empty because he didn't understand why this didn't make me feel loved. He was trying to show me love, but again, it was based on his love language and not mine. We are diving deep into the intimacy issues so many married couples struggle with in Chapter 12, so stay tuned. You are not alone if you are struggling in this area and I do not want to gloss over this very important piece of your marriage!

These classifications of "quality time" and "physical touch" are based on Gary Chapman's book, *The Five Love Languages*. He writes that the five love languages are: acts of service, quality time, gifts, words of affirmation, and physical touch.

Here's a quick breakdown for you! My guess is you can pinpoint right away which ones are yours and which ones are your husbands after reading the descriptions!

In no particular order:

- **Acts of Service:** You feel love when your spouse is doing something for you, helping out with chores, sharing responsibilities, and serving.

- **Quality Time:** You feel love by spending time together, just the two of you. Maybe it is a date, maybe it is just making supper together at home, but the key is that you are together.
- **Gifts**: You feel love when someone gets you a gift. It's not about the amount of money spent, but about the thought that goes behind the gift.
- **Words of Affirmation:** You feel loved by words. Spoken or written, you need to hear that you are loved.
- **Physical Touch:** You feel loved by being touched. Hugs, kisses, and sex itself would fall under this category. Intimacy can be communicated in a variety of different ways.

After reading Gary Chapman's book and taking the quiz, I learned that I receive love with acts of service first and foremost, and words of affirmation second. Meaning, you do the dishes for me, clean up the kids' toys, do a project I've been asking you to do, make a phone call to the electric company, or literally take anything off of my plate—you are my prince charming. If you go out of your way to write me a note or send me a text telling me you love me or that I'm beautiful, I'm putty in your hands.

Cody on the other hand, based on my observations of him, feels love with quality time. We don't have to be talking and we don't have to be doing anything at all—just my presence makes him feel loved. And he really loves it when I'm watching him do something that he's good at. It gives him a boost of confidence and he just likes to show off in front of me, I think. Which now that I know this…it's kind of cute. His other love language is gifts. He is seriously such a great gift giver and loves receiving gifts. My frugal behind and "never wanting to spend money side" definitely squashed this side of him. Finally, physical touch is one of Cody's love languages too. This happens to be common for most men, so I'm sure you are not surprised by that one.

Notice that I did not say, "Cody and I read this book together." No, no we did not. My husband wasn't into the personal development stuff. He wasn't into the growth mindset stuff, remember?

Shayla Huber

And even as I learned about the love languages and things started to click in my brain, I became more frustrated because I wasn't being loved in my love language. I wasn't sure how I was going to "get what I wanted" if he didn't also read the book and put in some effort. Have you ever felt like that? You just desperately want your husband to understand you and your needs and show some effort towards loving you better, but it all falls flat? If so, sister—it's okay! You are not alone; this is a common problem.

But what I realized is that I had to go first. If I was going to put this book into action and really see if it worked, I had to start showing Cody love in his love languages. I made the decision to work on my marriage and my part in it, and as much as I didn't want to admit it, my mother was right—two wrongs don't make a right. Keeping track of each other's love tank contribution was doing nothing for my sanity or peace and was actually spelling d-i-s-a-s-t-e-r for our marriage. Focusing on all of the ways that he was failing me just continued to divide us and in my mind I knew that it was not helping the situation at all.

I couldn't solve the problem on my own, but I could at least plug one hole in the dam. I was tired of being bitter and resentful, so I did something about it. I decided that it was worth it to spend more quality time with him in the barn. I started paying attention to little gifts I could get him or things that were out of the ordinary that he would appreciate, such as grabbing him a pop and hand delivering it to him (the old me would have never done such a thing)! Not only did I start spending more time with Cody, but I also started to listen to him more. You know how it is, sometimes we just have so much going on inside our heads we hear our husbands, but don't exactly listen. I often would forget the things he asked me or would be distracted by notifications on my phone instead of giving him my full attention. This really frustrated him and I was realizing just how inconsiderate I had been. God was slowly, but surely humbling me.

10 Things I Hate About My Husband

I'll never forget one day when I was working on my social media content for the week, and I had so many video ideas that I wanted to get done, plus I wanted to have time to go on a walk and work on this book too. Not to mention a couple of zoom calls scheduled. It was a packed day and as I sat down to get to work— my phone started to ring. It was Cody. He was asking me to come up to the shop and help him clean up a little bit. What do you think my response was?

Well, I immediately thought, *I do not have time for this. I just want to work on my own stuff today.* But there was also something nudging me that said *just go help him out.* So I did. I walked into his leather shop and grabbed a broom, and as he continued to cut out pieces of leather for some headstalls he was making, I swept the floor and moved some things around for him. After about 30 minutes of this, and very little conversation between the two of us, I was ready to go back to work. As I turned to leave, Cody thanked me for helping him and then reminded me that it was the anniversary of his grandfather's death. It had been two years since we lost him, and it was clear that Cody was missing him. His grandfather was his best friend and the one who passed the Leather Shop down to him.

In that moment, I was so thankful I had listened to the nudge to go help him. It wasn't my help Cody needed that day—it was my presence. I turned around and gave him a hug and a kiss and walked back to the house to finish up my work, glancing at the clock on my phone. Thirty minutes. It had only been thirty minutes. In that short period of time, I was able to fill my husband's love tank and show him love when he needed it most. What would have happened had I decided not to go help him? He may not have come home later that night and hugged me and helped me with the dishes. He may not have smiled and been present with his boys. He may have been distant and cold with me, instead of loving and helpful. What a difference speaking your spouse's love language can be!

But let me just tell you, making an effort for my husband, especially before he even made an effort—was super hard at first. It's hard to give and feel like you aren't getting anything back. But God tells us in 1 John 3:16: *"We know what real love is because Jesus gave up his life for us. So we also ought to give up our lives for our brothers and sisters."* And in verse 18: *"Dear children, let's not merely say that we love each other; let us show the truth by our actions."*

My logical brain could read these scriptures and know that God was calling me to love my husband unconditionally. But for some reason, my heart really struggled with it. Sometimes I felt like I was forcing it and shame and guilt would settle in because I didn't know why I couldn't be selfless like Jesus or the infamous woman in Proverbs 31.

In 1 John 4:7-8 it says: *"Dear friends, let us continue to love one another, for love comes from God. Anyone who loves is a child of God and knows God. But anyone who does not love does not know God, for God is love."* (NLT) Okay, this one hurts. This scripture, as a God-fearing Christian woman who is struggling to love her husband—really hits in all the right places. It convicts me of what God's love actually means. If you aren't loving others, then you truly do not know God. When I reflect on that time in my marriage, I was so caught up in my husband loving me the right way and seeing what I could get out of the marriage, I truly didn't know God's love. I had head knowledge, but not heart knowledge. And when you haven't experienced God's overwhelming, all-encompassing, never-ending love in your life, it's hard to know how to love others well.

Marriage is certainly not a walk in the park, it takes effort and the willingness to serve each other over ourselves. And if you aren't prepared for that, our selfish natures take over and it becomes all about "what's in it for me?" I had that mindset for way too long, and it eroded my marriage. But God. When He got a hold of me in a new way, I felt His love and had an identity shift. I saw

10 Things I Hate About My Husband

my husband in a completely new way. I began serving him and seeing him the way that God sees him—as a loved and chosen son of God. When I began to pursue God fervently and passionately, I began to learn more about how much He loves me. As I discovered for myself His true character, it became so much easier to love my husband! Instead of feeling like a chore, it felt like a natural overflow of love pouring out of me.

Recently, Cody and I along with our youngest son, Wacey, went out to check the cows. The night before, Cody had not had a good night in the roping pen. And it seemed like he woke up the next morning on the wrong side of the bed, still mad about it. He was grumpy and not his best self. The "pity-party" mentality was in full-swing. Usually, I would have said something along the lines of "snap out of it. It's a new day. Just get over it." His bad mood would have affected me negatively and my heart posture would have been annoyed at him for ruining my day. But this day was different.

I remember watching him driving the ranger and just admiring his chiseled face. I remember watching him check his deer blinds and finding him extremely attractive in his ball cap and blue jeans. I just remember watching him and being so full of love for him and it caught me off guard. He didn't do anything to deserve that kind of love. He actually, more than anything, pushed me away more than invited me into the moment.

And yet, I was overwhelmed with love for my husband.

"*This is what unconditional love feels like,*" I heard God whisper to me. "*This is my love overflowing in you and pouring out onto others. The love you feel for Cody right now is the love I feel for all of my children. It is not about what you do, how you act, or how bad you mess up. I love you and it is unconditional.*" With tears in my eyes, I sat there in awe of a God who has that kind of power and kindness and love for us humans. He who shows us mercy and grace.

At the end of the day, we are human. We are selfish sinners, and it is not always easy or natural to put another person's needs

90

in front of our own. It is not always easy to love someone on their worst day. But with God's love filling you up, it's possible. With God leading you and teaching you how to love, He gives us opportunities to show grace. He gives us opportunities to experience Him in all of his glory. John 15:12 says: *"This is my commandment: Love each other in the same way I have loved you."* (NLT)

If we were sitting across from each other at the coffee shop having a conversation right now, this is the part where I would grab your hand and remind you of a few powerful truths. I believe that your husband loves you very much. I believe he just doesn't know what he doesn't know. And I believe if you are willing to make the first move and learn how to love your husband in the way that speaks to him, it's because God has some growth planned for you. This is His invitation to live a Godly marriage, full of unconditional love. I believe that as you pursue God and experience His infinite love, you will learn to love your husband in a whole new way.

I understand some of you might be in a situation where you have been super hurt or wronged by your husband. Even betrayed. You have a lot of anger and frustration built up. Serving him and doing nice things for him might make you feel literally nauseous right now. Talking about unconditional love might feel like the hardest thing you could ever imagine doing and you want to throw this book across the room right now.

I want to remind you that there is nothing wrong with feeling this way. You aren't being selfish, you are hurt, and that's ok. Your emotions matter, including the hurt and pain that you are carrying. I want to highly encourage you to seek counseling first and foremost. With your husband or without him, seek wise Godly counsel around your marriage. When unforgiveness continues to fester inside of you, it's more harmful for you than it is for the other person. It's not only toxic; it's deadly. We are called to forgive, just like God forgives us. He sent Jesus to die for our sins so that we would be forgiven. So that we would have eternity with

Him! And if we are called to be more like Jesus, we are called to forgive. Even when it's hard.

Living in unforgiveness and hurt is one way that Satan likes to destroy marriages. He tells us that there is no getting past it, and there is no use in trying. But remember who ultimately is victorious at the end of the day—Christ.

It might feel hopeless at this moment, but don't let Satan win. All is not lost. The very fact that you are reading this book, specifically this chapter shows that you have a small glimmer of hope inside of you that desires to love your husband better and learn how to forgive him. I can't promise you it's going to be easy—but I can promise you it's going to be worth it. Redemption is possible. Restoration can be yours. God's power and authority are so much greater than the enemy's lies and schemes. God provides freedom through forgiveness, love, and grace and he has all of that for you and more in your life and in your marriage.

SCRIPTURE:

Ephesians 4:30-32 (NLT)

"And do not bring sorrow to God's Holy Spirit by the way you live. Remember, he has identified you as his own, guaranteeing that you will be saved on the day of redemption. Get rid of all bitterness, rage, anger, harsh words, and slander, as well as all types of evil behavior. Instead, be kind to each other, tenderhearted, forgiving one another, just as God through Christ has forgiven you."

PRAYER:

Father God, thank you for the knowledge of the 5 love languages. God, you know my heart and you know my story. I do not want to be self-seeking and prideful in my marriage, I want to be kind and giving. I do not want to live in unforgiveness and hurt, but I want to walk in the freedom that only you provide. Help me to model what a healthy and loving marriage is for our children. Continue to teach me about unconditional love. Armor me with patience, trust and perseverance as I continue to fight for and honor my husband and marriage. Amen.

QUESTIONS:

1. What is your love language?
2. What is your husband's love language?
3. Is there unforgiveness that you are holding on to that you can see is causing a divide between you and your husband?
4. What does unconditional love look like and feel like for you?

10 Things I Hate About My Husband

SOMETHING TO TRY: *The Cookie Jar*

When the timing feels right and you want to try something to expand on the love languages, the cookie jar is a fun idea! It takes the guesswork out for both you and your husband when trying to decide how to "fill the love tank" of each other. I learned this from the book, *Sex Begins in the Kitchen* by Dr. Kevin Leman. When I brought it up to Cody, he seemed reluctant, but also a little excited!

Take two different pieces of paper, one identifies as his and one identifies as yours. And the two of you write down different things you want from the other. For example, I may write down that I want a massage, I want him to plan and make supper, or I want to watch a movie together. All on different slips of paper. Cody may write that he wants me to make him a cheesecake, go hunting with him, or go out on a date to his favorite steakhouse. The key is to focus on what would fill your love tank. Then once a week (or once a month depending on how often you can remember), you choose a slip from the jar. Whatever the slip of paper says, that is what you do for your spouse! Again, this takes the guesswork out and both of you end up getting something that you've been wanting, without the nagging or pressure that can sometimes come with this kind of stuff. It truly is a win-win and you learn more about the other in the process!

7.

Communication

Hi, my name is Shayla and I like to talk. Like, a lot. I am a total "Chatty Kathy." At any point in time, you can find me chatting with the cashier at the grocery store, a mom during Wednesday night youth group, or a friend on my iPhone as I do laps on our circle drive in front of our house. Unfortunately, I've missed multiple calf roping runs of my husbands because I was too busy chatting to the wife sitting next to me in the bleachers to even hear Cody's name over the loudspeaker. Whoops.

Most of the time I go from small talk about the weather, to discussing my kids, to the deeper meaning of life and what God has been teaching me. You hang around me for too long, we are going to get deep really quick and talk about God's truth. I don't like to sugarcoat or beat around the bush and I tend to share my heart and soul openly. You come to me with a problem, heads up that we most likely are going to find a solution through Jesus Christ. I genuinely love people and want them to know they are loved, seen, and special. But I do consider myself an "extroverted introvert." Meaning that I'm filled up when I'm around people and tend to be a social butterfly, but I also need time alone to recharge. I'm like a cell phone. I talk and talk and talk until my battery runs out, then I need to be plugged in to charge.

My husband, on the other hand, does not share my gift of gab. While I am a woman of many words, he is a man of few words. There have been times where I've attempted to have a heartfelt conversation with him and... crickets. Like, "Hello! Did you even hear me? I'm baring my soul over here!" Or there are times where I wanted us to discuss the coming week, like what is going on with our kids, plans for supper, or projects I wanted to get done…and again, radio silence. Communication is such a vital component to any relationship; I would worry myself sick about the lack thereof in our own marriage. I began to believe we were headed for doomsday if my husband didn't pick it up a little bit in this department.

Now, I am not here to stereotype genders. I'm not here to say all men are terrible communicators and all women over-communicate. But the fact that I was (and still am) an over-communicator, and he was (and still is) an under-communicator felt like the end of the world to me. And I would be hard-pressed to find no other married couple to have this same problem.

Maybe it's your schedules that are not clear and so things continually get missed during the week. "I didn't know Leroy had a T-ball game tonight and I already told so-so they could come over to rope tonight." Maybe it's the constant "what's for supper" conversation that drives you absolutely bonkers and you just want to have it planned out. "I don't care babe, what do you want to have?" *Gah! Just tell me what to fix for supper!*

Or maybe it's that you truly are ships passing each other at night and you are totally missing all communication with each other, leading you to feel disconnected and lonely. There is no time for date nights, breakfast together, or even brushing your teeth at the same time before bed because life is just that busy. This seems to be the beginning stages of what people would say "we started drifting apart." There are no talks about the future, no discussions about dreams, and no tender-hearted, sweet-nothings whispered in each other's ears. Mostly, it's just quiet, and quiet is a dangerous place to be.

So, whether it's everyday communication that a marriage needs to help a house and family function, or it's the deeper, heartfelt conversations that you and your husband are missing, I think the nuggets I'm sharing in this chapter will resonate with you!

Shayla Huber

What can great communication do for your marriage? How can it help the flow of your home and create more peace and harmony amongst the chaos and noise? I have a few practical tips to get your communication started off on the right foot.

The first thing that my husband and I have implemented is working together on our schedules. We both are self-employed, so we work from home. Our 5-year-old, Leroy, is in full-time kindergarten and our 2-year-old, Wacey, goes to daycare three days a week. Cody knows the days that I am in "work-mode" and he knows the days I'm "full-time mommy mode." Conversely, I know the days that Cody is going to be gone or the days he is going to be working in his leather shop. We know who is doing drop off and pick-up with the boys and generally what is happening most nights. The more we can have it planned ahead of time, the better we both are because we are sticking to our intentions.

If I were to randomly tell Cody I need him to take the boys because something pops up and he's already loading up the truck to take a load of calves somewhere—it would most likely cause unnecessary stress and chaos. Of course, there are exceptions thanks to our flexible schedules (and the boys love loading up in the truck to go anywhere with their dad). But you get the idea. There have been many days my work gets interrupted because I need to help Cody get a lost calf back in the pen or he needs help loading hay in his trailer. That's the beauty of farm life for you. But generally speaking, there are kids' activities, birthday parties, rodeos, family stuff, and work stuff all happening in the span of a week. And I swear, the more you can communicate about what is going on the better! Maybe like us, it's time to get a calendar and label it the "family calendar" and write down everything on it so nothing gets lost!

This was something that Cody used to be really annoyed with. He keeps everything going on in his mind and I truly need to write it down or else I will miss it. (Again, two totally different brains here). He didn't understand why I wanted to write down his rodeos on the calendar or why I would always ask him what he had going on that day. Flying by the seat of our pants might have worked decently before kids, but not anymore. There are just too many responsibilities and too much going on. As someone who is bound and determined to be a team with my husband (remember the vision God gave me), I decided I would work on this side of communicating, regardless of his attitude about it. So as gruffy as his responses were sometimes, I wrote out his monthly plans and discussed with him mine. And slowly, but surely, Cody picked up on the benefits of planning ahead. He saw that our home functioned better, that I was less stressed, and that our kids seemed happier, too!

Even if your husband doesn't see the potential in communicating about the necessities and he's more of a "fly-by-the-seat-of-your-pants" guy, I promise you, he may come around to it. Stay patient. Now Cody is the one making sure I know what's going on and writing appointments on the calendar! Teamwork makes the dream work!

Another helpful tool in my communicator's toolbelt has been a menu board to plan our weekly meals. When we're able to do this for the upcoming week, I feel on top of the world. I save so much time not having to think about what to make, and not to mention we save money by using ingredients we have on hand already! I don't know if I'm just happy because I'm saving time and money—but the food tends to taste better too! When we do this as a team, I know I'm making food that Cody actually wants and I end up making different meals week to week, instead of always the same ten rotations. We all know how boring that gets!

I believe having crystal-clear communication about every day things is what makes it possible to have open communication about the harder things. There are situations where lack of communication from your husband stings a bit more. He comes home from work and heads straight to his chair to watch television. You watch him engage with the kids for all of five minutes, and then he's entranced on his phone. You go to share something about your day and instead of offering encouragement or feedback, he shrugs his shoulders and says, "I see." You walk back to the kitchen feeling depleted, uncared for, and even disrespected. He's not filling up your words of affirmation love tank in the slightest. You feel like he doesn't even care about you. *What a jerk*, you think to yourself. It's in these moments you may even feel invisible to him and just want to cry.

Listen, I've been there. And if you want, you can let your mind go crazy. You can choose to believe all of the stories that are rushing through your head. *He doesn't even love me. He's a terrible husband and father. He's so selfish. I deserve better than this. This isn't what I signed up for.* On and on we go around the merry-go-round. Remember, these are thoughts. On the outside it may look like total truth and the enemy that wants to divide you and your husband is going to make them look as truthful as the spaghetti cooking on your stove. But the reality is that you truly don't know what he's thinking about either. You don't know what kind of day he had either. Is the lack of communication hurting the both of you? Yes. But the stories in your head are hurting the situation more and it's time we learn how to shut them up once and for all.

I used to listen to these thoughts and believe the stories I told myself about Cody. Funny thing is, the more I was convinced that the story I was telling myself was true, the more miserable I would become. After pouting in the kitchen, crying into the spaghetti, and letting the thoughts grow louder and louder in my mind—I would erupt. I yelled, screamed, cussed, slammed doors, nagged and did anything in a desperate attempt to get my way. In a desperate attempt to get my husband to open up to me and talk to me. But all that did was set our relationship to "roller coaster" mode. We would ride all the highs and lows together when we would get in a big fight and then make up afterwards. It was such a vicious cycle. This was what communication looked like in our house. I mean, we both are super passionate and enthusiastic people. Maybe this was just our personalities at work? Are we just like oil and fire? I honestly wasn't sure and my brain was exhausted. But eventually, I got to the point where I wanted off the roller coaster.

God is love and we can be confident that when our thoughts are not filled with love, it's not from Him. God unites, so we can be sure that when our thoughts are filled with division, it's not from Him. God shows mercy and grace and forgiveness to sinners, and so when our thoughts are filled with hatred and anger towards a spouse who is a sinner, we can be confident those thoughts are not from Him. Our sinful humanness shines through when we are feeling depleted in our relationship and the enemy loves nothing more than to grab a hold of us in these vulnerable states to capitalize on division, hatred, and fighting. He loves nothing more than to keep you believing you are a victim in this situation and there is no light at the end of the tunnel.

Maybe you grew up witnessing a lot of fighting and verbal head-to-head matches. Maybe you didn't learn how to communicate with an inside voice. Maybe your husband was raised to keep his feelings inside, or that it is better to be seen than heard. Maybe during the day there were no fights between your parents, but on the other side of the wall, when you were supposed to be asleep in the middle of the night, you could hear the disagreements and the arguing of your parents who wanted to protect you from seeing the hard part of marriage.

Our pasts, our traumas, and how we were raised all shape how we show up in our marriage. And at the end of the day, my cussing and yelling was not about my husband being a terrible communicator. It was about my heart screaming to be heard and understood. It was about the thoughts and stories I believed to be true by an enemy looking to destroy. It was about a heart looking to be healed by a human being who was never meant to be her savior after all.

Shayla Huber

When I began to take ownership of my thoughts and I began to take responsibility for my part of the marriage, things started to change. When I started to take every thought captive and make it obedient to Christ, things started to change. When I started to challenge myself and instead of being consumed with my own thoughts, I started to get curious about my husband, things started to change. Sure, I haven't heard something nice spoken to me in awhile, but when was the last time I said something nice to Cody? When was the last time I greeted him with a smile instead of a frown? When was the last time I listened to him without being distracted on my phone? What can I give that I have not been giving?

Ladies, it's okay to take the first step. Write him a note, send him a text, or write on the whiteboard on the fridge something you appreciate about him. This may come as a shock to his system, but even if words of affirmation are not his thing—it will get his attention. The truth is our men want to be filled up too. They want to know if we care about them. They want to feel seen. They may be filled with thoughts around being a disappointment or failure to you and one small step towards debunking that lie could mean the world to him.

Ephesians 4:29 tells us: "*And never let ugly or hateful words come from your mouth, but instead let your words become beautiful gifts that encourage others; do this by speaking words of grace to help them.*" I, for one, was not exuding beautiful gifts out of my mouth. I was aiming arrows of fire right at my husband because it was all about me. I was so hyper-focused on finding the negativity in my husband and the hurt that I was feeling inside. I just wanted something to make me feel better and was continuing to look for the solution in people, things, and circumstances.

And ladies, it isn't always about me. And it isn't always about you. Marriage is designed to make us holy. Marriage is designed to make us more like Jesus. I'm not saying it doesn't stink to have a communication problem, because it does. I'm not saying it doesn't stink to go to bed at night feeling lonely, because it does. But we have got to understand that there is life and death in the power of our tongue.

Proverbs 18:21 says: *"The tongue can bring death or life; those who love to talk will reap the consequences."* (NLT) There is power in what you say to your husband and you can be speaking life or you can be speaking death. There is power in our thoughts. And we can either believe what the world says…which usually points us to giving up when things get hard. Or we can believe what God says. His Word truthfully says: *"You can pray for anything, and if you have faith, you will receive it."* (Matthew 21:22 NLT)

I spent way too many years listening to the devil's whispers about my husband's flaws, and what I thought I was entitled to. I listened to his temptations that I would be happier if: If we had more money, if we communicated better, or if he loved me better. Those thoughts only lead us towards more fighting, more destruction, and more hopelessness. Exactly where the enemy wants you.

I was sick and tired of feeling like my husband didn't understand me. I was sick and tired of making up stories about what he was thinking and what he wasn't doing right. I was sick and tired of not having a vibrant and intentional marriage. I was sick and tired of doubting that this man was the one for me and just going through the motions. I was sick and tired of believing the enemy's lies that were bound and determined to divide my husband and I, so I set out to disarm the enemy.

When I finally realized my authority in Jesus Christ, as a loved daughter of God, it shut the enemy up. Stepping into my identity in Christ and learning how to let God fight for me, literally changed everything about my marriage. Everything changed about my thoughts, my words, my behavior, my demeanor. I decided to stop playing victim and started playing the victor. I started speaking out, "I'm victorious! I am a loved and chosen daughter of God and I know my place in this marriage. I know who I am and what I have to offer and I'm going to show up like Jesus from now on. Everything I pray for with the fullness of faith I will receive and I am praying for a beautiful and loving marriage!" That may sound silly, but the enemy cowers at truthful declarations spoken out loud.

By putting my own pride aside, God graciously began changing my heart. By seeking God first and learning more about His true character, he taught me about unconditional love. By facing my past and the heart wounds that I still was holding on to, God completely changed me. I don't know the last time I slammed a door in my husband's face. I don't remember the last time I swore at him or called him names or yelled, and that's because I'm different. I'm no longer the same Shayla, I'm a new creation in Christ. The Holy Spirit has taken root and now shines through me. 2 Corinthians 5:17 describes it perfectly: *"This means that anyone who belongs to Christ has become a new person. The old life is gone; a new life has begun!"*

Do I still get upset sometimes when his responses back to me are one word answers after I just poured my heart out? Yes. Do I still feel frustrated sometimes when the days are long and we had no time to actually talk that day? Sure. Do I still fight my earthly flesh and have to think really hard about my response when he leaves a mess in the kitchen? Of course! But my tone of voice has changed. My demeanor has changed. My mindset has changed. I think before speaking, ask instead of nag, and run to my Heavenly Father for support and guidance.

I have grace for my husband when I used to have judgment. I have patience when I used to be easily irritated. I don't expect my husband to be anything but who he is and I love and appreciate him for what he does bring to the table. I stopped taking so many things personally and I stopped believing the enemy's lies. Both of our needs are being met in ways that I used to dream about and our home is full of peace, love, and joy again.

10 Things I Hate About My Husband

Communication is serious stuff. And I'm sure there is a plethora of strategies and tips you can adopt to help you and your husband. There might even be specific prompts you can print out and use! But for me, getting to the deeper issue as to why I was yelling, what thoughts I was thinking, and why I was believing them were the true key to unlocking great communication with my husband. Allowing God to transform my heart and begin to heal the voids that I was feeling helped me to silence the lies and show up with more care, love, and softness. Instead of white knuckling the fruits of the spirit, they started to flow out of me! And that my friends, is the true work of Jesus Christ. Can I get an Amen?

We'll be diving so much deeper into heart healing and transformation in the chapters to come, but for now, go write your husband a love note and tell him what you love about him! Don't worry if it feels weird or that it will catch him off guard. Just do it!

SCRIPTURE:
Proverbs 18:20 (NLT)
"Wise words satisfy like a good meal; the right words bring satisfaction."

PRAYER:
Father, thank you for the gift of communication. Our words have so much power and can either hurt or heal. Forgive me for all of the hurtful things I have said to my husband. Help me to show him grace and love as we work towards better communication in our marriage. Help me to use my voice for GOOD and to focus on all the things I love about my husband. Amen.

QUESTIONS:

1. What is a practical communication tool you want to try this week?
2. What lie are you going to lay down about your husband so that you can start to see him the way that God sees him?
3. Have you felt shame or guilt around yelling, screaming, etc. and are ready to understand yourself on a deeper level? Ask God to reveal to you what is inside of your heart and what emotions come up when you yell. What are the deeper needs you are trying to communicate?

8.
Single Mommin' It

I titled Chapter 1, "Cowboy Dreams," because I know I'm not the only woman alive who dreamed about a cowboy taking her away. (Thanks a lot, Dixie Chicks.) I mean, you have your type, right? There is nothing I find sexier than my husband dressed in his starched Cinch jeans and belt buckle. Whether he's going to a rodeo or he's going to the back to check cows, I find him extremely attractive. But more than how he looks, it's how he carries himself that really gets me. It's the calm patience he has when working with a young horse. It's the intense focus when having to rope a calf in the pasture. It's the friendly midwestern wave as he passes a truck on the gravel road. It's the values that he represents, including honesty, hard work, and passion. Cowboys put the needs of their livestock ahead of their own. They are always there to lend a hand to a neighbor or to someone who broke down on the side of the road. All these qualities and more represent my husband, and it's what made me fall in love with him in the first place.

However, what Dixie Chicks failed to mention in their hit song is that "cowboy take me away" is the precedent to "cowboy will be gone and you'll be left at home for long periods of time." I personally would have really appreciated a more realistic sequel to one of my favorite songs. But I digress. One thing I didn't quite consider before saying "I do" to my cowboy was the amount of time that my husband would be gone. When I say gone, it could mean gone for a whole week or two on the rodeo trail. The longest we have ever gone without seeing each other is a month! Or it could mean he's home, but he has a million things to do in the span of 24 hours and so he's gone from our physical house for the day. I don't want to say it's never ending, but it really is. There are chores in the morning and chores at night. During the day there is leather work, roping, checking cows, or fixing fences.

There is always something to do, and Cody doesn't relax well. He's always on the move, always working on something. Not to mention all of the "emergencies" that farm wives and ranch wives are all too familiar with like cows getting out, neighbors needing assistance, or broken-down-tractors. You get the idea. He's gone—a lot.

On one hand, there are husbands who are physically gone often. And on the other hand, there are husbands who are just emotionally or mentally withdrawn. In this scenario you may feel like roommates—maybe even like strangers. He may come home from work, head straight to his chair in front of the tv, and maybe rumble some caveman response to your greeting. This can feel as hard or even harder than your husband not being there physically.

Either way, if this is you, I think you will resonate so much with this topic. You are going to resonate feeling like a single mom even though you are not. In fact, you feel like you are doing everything by yourself. From getting the kids ready for school or daycare, working all day (whether at a job or at home as a stay-at-home-mom), cooking, cleaning, grocery shopping, bills, and keeping track of all of the appointments and games for your family—it's a lot to juggle. And when you slow down long enough to actually sit down, you are overcome with exhaustion, overwhelm, resentment, and anger towards a spouse who doesn't seem to be fulfilling their end of the bargain. You feel incredibly alone, like the world is on your shoulders and if you take one wrong step, the whole house is going to come crashing down.

As I told you before, one of the most motivating things about starting a business from home was so that I could take it with me and I wouldn't have to work a 9-5. I had gotten used to Cody's busy schedule and wanted to find something that would fit in with his lifestyle. The rodeo season officially starts in October and ends late September. The busiest times for him are winter rodeos in the South, the summer run, and then some finals in the fall. When we were just a family of three it was pretty easy to pack up and go. Leroy was born in April and by June we were full-time rodeo and on the road. We were gone so much back then that I had to write out our utility bills a month in advance so my mother-in-law could get them sent in the mail for us! We were living out our vision and it was wonderful. But then, along came Wacey Eugene.

Our second little cowboy joined us October 28th, 2021, just two days before Cody had a huge roping to attend. Our family of four was complete. Cody rushed off to the roping in Texas the day after Wacey was born. I didn't love the way it felt being driven home by my mom instead of my husband, but I was eager to get home so we could at least watch him on TV at the roping and I was super appreciative to have my mom with me. Looking back now, I wonder if that day was a foreboding picture of the hardships that were to come over the next year.

Picture this. We just got home from the hospital. I'm settled into our recliner, soaking in the snuggles and newborn baby smells of my sweet Wacey, as Leroy is running around the house with excitement, trying on his Halloween costume for us to see. We are so cozy in our blanket as the fall weather starts settling in deeper and the leaves continue to fly in the wind. Home feels like the best place in the world—we are just missing our daddy.

And as we watch him rope on TV, he's doing real good. He backs in the box with only one more run to make it back to the short round. His calf takes off, his horse Rudy starts running as fast as he can, Cody ropes his calf, sharp as can be… and next thing I know, I'm watching my husband get drug around the arena because his foot is caught in the stirrup. The cameraman immediately takes the camera off of the action, and I'm left to imagine what is happening beyond the screen.

During that time about 20 other cowboys charge the scene,

cut Cody's rope, and make sure he and Rudy are okay. I was devastated. This meant he would be coming home with no money, a bummed out knee, and most likely, a defeated spirit. He was already sad and guilty about having to leave early and miss going home with us from the hospital. Now he didn't even have anything to show for it, to make the trip worthwhile. But regardless, I was so thankful he was going to be okay and would be coming home soon. This was the beginning scene of the absolute chaos that was about to unfold in my life over the next few months.

When Wacey was just two weeks old, we went to the Great Lakes Circuit Finals Rodeo in Louisville, KY, a place we affectionately call our home away from home. It felt great to be supporting Cody as a new family, and I had so many visions of what our life was going to look like from then on. Long drives in the truck with the boys sleeping peacefully as we headed to the next rodeo. Cody taking Leroy with him to check on the arena and calves, while I stayed at the trailer to nurse Wacey and get everything put back together from our travels. Dressing my boys in cute western shirts and sitting in the stands, cheering loud for daddy. I thought to myself, *I've been through postpartum life once before, I can do this again. It was easy taking Leroy on the road when he was little, this will be a piece of cake. I'm supporting my mental wellness through natural supplements now…I'm focusing on my health and rest. I've grown so much over the past 2 years with my mindset — I can do this.*

Wrong. I was so wrong. My postpartum journey with Wacey was ten times harder than it was with Leroy. It would take me a full two hours to get this child to go to sleep because every time I laid him on his back, he would scream. The only time he would actually sleep was on my chest or on his belly. Naps were the same way. It would take me hours to lay him down. My baby carrier became my best friend, and Wacey spent most of his day strapped in with me. He really did love it and we had all the bonding time we needed.

This kid. He was just fussy all the dang time! I started researching all the things about having a colicky baby that I could find and started trying different things. I tried the gas drops. I got him on an infant probiotic. I tried to avoid milk and other foods that could trigger a breastfed baby with colic. Thankfully, I had a ton of support from friends who had gone through the same thing, offering suggestions, but things just didn't get better. I was so worn out that most days I stayed in my sweatpants, hair in a messy ponytail, and went through the motions of just trying to survive one more day. I did my best to keep showing up with energy for my boys, for Cody and for my business, but things were definitely taking a toll.

It all came to a head when Wacey was around five months old, and I was at my wits end with sleep deprivation. I decided to ask my doctor if he could possibly have reflux. My gut told me he was in more pain than just being fussy. He had to be propped up to sleep (you should have seen his bassinet. It literally looked like a cocoon). And half the time I just drove him around because sleeping in his car seat was the only comfortable thing for him besides my carrier. I'll never forget having an important business presentation one night, preparing for it in my head as I drove my baby around town, laughing at the absurdity of it all.

There was one night in particular that I remember crying out to the Lord for help. I didn't feel equipped to take care of my baby. I was so exhausted and worn down. Cody was gone so much that it was up to me to juggle both kids by myself. I felt like I was neglecting Leroy every single night because I had to put him in front of the tv so I could try and get Wacey to go down. My heart was torn in two every time I told Leroy I was sorry for not being able to spend more time with him and he always said, "It's okay, Momma." In my professional life, I felt like my business was taking a back seat and I was not the leader I wanted to be. It was hard. I felt God's presence that night, comforting me and holding me, and I believe it was the beginning of a greater surrender that he was preparing for me.

10 Things I Hate About My Husband

The doctor finally diagnosed him as having reflux and my instinct had been right! Moms, this is your sign to trust your gut when it comes to your kids! You truly do know when something is off, so don't be afraid to advocate for yourself, your babies, and ask questions! Things improved greatly after we started him on a low dose of medicine and a reflux specific formula. His tummy felt so much better and he instantly improved with less crying and more smiles. We all started sleeping again, and he was so much happier. He didn't need to be carried so much. It felt like I was able to experience the fun milestones with him now, instead of only being focused on the hard stuff.

And because I wasn't so sleep-deprived, my mental health started improving. My mental focus and clarity returned, my energy was better, and it just felt like I could breathe easier. I was able to spend so much more intentional time with Leroy before his own bedtime, instead of barely getting through one book before passing out with exhaustion.

During those really hard months, dealing with the undiagnosed reflux and new mom life to two boys, Cody had five or six total rodeo trips, with some lasting a week at a time. If there was ever a time I felt like a single mom, it was during that season of my life. Being sleep deprived, having postpartum hormones, and being alone and stressed is the perfect combination for a storm to happen. And I knew it. I was very aware of my past resentments around supporting Cody's dreams and not being able to pursue mine actively. I was very aware that the situation we were in was out of our control and we were both just doing the best that we could with me holding down the home front and Cody providing for our family. Even though I desperately wanted to be on the road with Cody, I didn't think I could mentally handle living in a horse trailer with all of Wacey's issues. It all felt like too much and I was in complete survival mode. With a touch of crazy.

Even though I tried so hard to not let my emotions take over, they did. Even though I tried to not make Cody feel guilty for being gone so much, I did. Even though I kept telling myself how strong I am and that I can do this, I still felt so defeated half the time and that I really was not equipped to handle motherhood. One minute I was thinking, *I'm strong. I can do this. I knew that this is what I was signing up for.* And then the next minute I thought, *Who am I kidding. I can't do this. I am in way over my head. I can't take another day like this. If only Cody was home, it would be easier.* I was "in the thick of it" as people like to say, and it was rough. I saw myself as the yelling, screaming, hard-to-please wife that I had been working so hard to leave in the past and the shame was choking me. More times than not, if you would have knocked on my door during those days to visit, you would have found me in my closet, crying my eyes out, holding Wacey in my arms, googling ways to help my baby feel better.

It is in these super hard moments that it can be so easy to resent our husbands for being gone. I see TikTok videos all the time of marriages being broken over moms feeling like single moms and deciding to call it quits. They say things like, "I'm still a single mom, but now I don't have anyone to answer to. I'm still a single mom, it's just now actually official." This both frustrates and saddens me.

What they are saying is that it is so much better that they got a divorce because they had no help in the first place. I don't know the ins and outs of those relationships, but I do know that the videos break my heart. I do know that the kids in those relationships are going to have to exchange parents in the McDonald's parking lot every week or two. I do know that the repercussions of this decision can produce more division in the generations to come—even though in the moment it felt like walking away was the only option. I do know that God is bigger than any broken marriage and can redeem any person. And I do know that it is worth it to lean on Him for support when you feel utterly alone, lost, and depleted.

I'm coming at this from the point of view of *I know how*

hard it is. I know how frustrating it can be to have friends or people on social media who have husbands who are home every single night at 5:00 pm. I remember the jealousy and the longing of wishing I had that, too. They cook, clean, spend extra time with the kids and it seems like your family unit is broken and extremely lacking this magical touch. It seems unfair for you to have the extra load of work or you just flat out miss your husband. You miss his hugs, his voice, his presence. You desperately want him there tucking your kids into bed, making sure the doors are locked, and snuggling in close to you as he gets into bed. You want a teammate and a partner to do life with and that's the furthest thing from what you have right now.

It was the furthest thing from what I had, and that anger from his absence turned into bitterness. Then the bitterness turned into pride. Sadly, I fell victim to the cultural narrative that said, "I can do it all" and it left me miserable, broken, stressed, and with a strained marriage. I fell victim to believing I had something to prove to the world, so I needed to do everything and everything well—especially because my husband was gone a lot.

I had this internal need to be valued and seen based on my works. The more I appeared like I had it all together, that I was successful, and that I didn't need anyone, the better. I even pushed my husband away when he did try to help because he didn't do anything the way that I did, so it was easier to just do it myself. I became overly controlling of many things, which cost me unnecessary worry and anxiety.

From the dishes being done right, to how to parent my children, to the plans we made, it was my way or the highway. That kind of living is suffocating! What God has been graciously teaching me is that my control was actually rooted in fear. Fear that said God was far away from me and didn't truly love me so I needed to do everything on my own. Fear that everything would fall apart if I didn't do it myself. Fear that if I didn't do this whole work-from-home-mom life perfectly—then I wouldn't find success and overall happiness. This type of fear was overriding any kind of freedom that God was wanting to give me. The fear and control was putting my faith and trust in myself and worldly circumstances instead of in my Heavenly Father. The fear looked like a prideful, controlling, and stressed-out mom who was ready to pull her hair out.

Philippians 4:6-7 says: *"Don't worry about anything; instead, pray about everything. Tell God what you need and thank him for all he has done. Then you will experience God's peace, which exceeds anything we can understand. His peace will guard your hearts and minds as you live in Christ Jesus."* (NLT)

It is His peace that will bring you freedom. It is His peace that will give you strength for the days you are alone. It is His peace that will help you set down pride and control and the need for approval because at the end of the day, God's the one in charge and He wants to come alongside you in life to help you. To take care of you. And to provide for you. God was not changing my husband's occupation any time soon. But He was changing my heart. And through changing my heart, and accepting that which I cannot control, he provided solutions to help get through the hard reality of feeling like a single mom.

The first of which is to not be afraid to ask for help. There truly is an epidemic of burnt-out, stressed out, overworked moms. Just like me, so many moms fall into that prideful trap of "I can do it all." Here is the thing. I do not believe God created moms to have to work from sunup to sundown with zero support and zero time for herself. Have you heard the phrase that says, "it takes a village?" Well, that's because it used to be that way. Moms used to have help from extended family, it was well received and there was community behind raising children.

Psalm 127:2-3 says: *"It is useless for you to work so hard from early morning until late at night, anxiously working for food to eat; for God gives rest to his loved ones. Children are a gift from the Lord; they are a reward from him."* (NLT)

10 Things I Hate About My Husband

Notice how He calls us to rest in one verse and in the next reminds us that children are a gift from God! He doesn't want us working from sun-up to sun-down. He wants us enjoying our babies and raising our families. Instead of mothers running around with their hair on fire, hustling to get the kids out the door, hustling to work, sprinting into the grocery store, throwing food at their kids for supper before rushing out the door to go to a multitude of events and then everyone collapsing in bed before doing it all again the next day…

I see a well-rested and energetic mom who is able to get up before the kids to spend time with Jesus and to prepare for the day. I see her getting breakfast made and lunches packed and then greeting her kids with hugs and smiles when they wake up. I see her pursuing her God-given calling with purpose and joy and fulfillment, with time to stop and smell the roses. I see her doing things with her family like playing in the yard after school, making bubble faces during bath time, and reading multiple books as she cuddles with her babies before bedtime. I see a mom who lives a slow and intentional life because she doesn't give in to the cultural narrative.

This rapid fire society, built around busyness, success, and a "more is better" attitude has driven us so far away from God's original design for family. Keep the husband away working long hours, believing that his role in the family is not as meaningful as the mom's. Keep the mom busy so that she doesn't have time to slow down, sit down, or even think, so her role becomes that of a dictator or coach, instead of as a nurturing and loving mother that she wants to be.

It all feels so backwards, and I believe it is one way that the enemy sneakily attacks. Keep us so busy that we can't see straight. Keep us so busy that we aren't intentionally raising our kids, we are skating by, using technology or outside influences to do the teaching for us. Keep us so busy, that husbands and wives don't have time for each other, to grow and foster a marriage based on love and trust.

As you can see, pride, hustle culture, and a distant husband is the breeding ground for a miserable wife. It's the perfect storm for the enemy to attack. But what would happen if we looked up and gave ourselves permission to ask for help? What would happen if we put our pride aside, asked for help, and truly started breathing again?

I am very blessed to have my mom, who is retired, living only a couple of hours away, and my mother-in-law who is actually my next door neighbor. (She comes in real handy when I'm needing a cup of sugar)! These two are the lucky women I call when I need help. Whether it is having my mother-in-law pick up something for me while she is in town to save me a trip, or having my mom take the kids for a weekend, they truly have been a Godsend on this motherhood journey. When my mom comes to visit, she does the laundry and helps do little projects around the house we haven't gotten to yet. If I have a last minute zoom call and Cody is nowhere to be found, my Mother-in-law will take the boys for me. They truly want to help and I hope to be able to do the same for my own children someday. This is the "it takes a village" piece. But the key part of all of this is accepting the help. Laying the pride down and receiving it. I don't have to do it all and God hasn't designed me to do it all. And the same goes for you.

In Matthew 11:30, Jesus says: *"For my yoke is easy to bear, and the burden I give you is light."* (NLT) God is able to walk with us through anything. He is able to give us strength when we are weak. He can pair his super with our natural in times of struggle, and He is with us in the chaos, too. But we can hear him more clearly in the rest. We can hear Him more clearly in the silence. And when we ask for help, take time to recharge our batteries, and seek God more closely during those precious moments—He will bless that obedience and trust.

When I decided to ditch the hustle, slow down my life, and actively pursue God first, He revealed to me His true character of love. He revealed to me my true identity as His daughter—and it

117

changed everything for my home and marriage. It changed everything about the direction of my life. When I am able to be filled back up, live presently and intentionally, and allow others to love on my children too, my kids get a happier mom and a happier home. When I drop the control, I'm showing myself and God that I'm putting my trust in Him to lead me and meet my needs so I can meet the needs of others.

NOTE: If you don't have a mom or mother-in-law because of death, distance, or some other extenuating circumstance, I'm praying over that void for you right now. Moms are such an important part of our lives and if anyone is missing that piece of them, my heart goes out to you. I encourage you, if you're comfortable with this, and maybe even if you're not—reflect on that hurt and ask God what he wants to heal in your heart. Ask him where that void is coming up in your own life and trust that God is working all things out for your good.

Asking for help has also allowed me to pursue my God-given calling beyond motherhood. I know that God has called me to be both a mother and a businesswoman (and an author as you are holding this book). God has called me to speak into women's lives about His truth, His love, and His healing work. And it is something I am crazy passionate about!

Megan is part of my village, too. Having part-time daycare help from Megan, an amazing mother and friend, has given me the opportunity to create the space in my life to pursue these callings. Wacey gets to play with friends a few days a week, and Momma gets to work and pour into others! But I also have the flexibility to keep him home when I want to, be there when my kids are sick, or even help Cody on the farm if he needs me.

As long as my priorities are God, Cody, Boys, Business, God creates the space and time I need to pursue what He has laid on my heart! That's the kind of freedom He wants to give to all of

His children. No matter what you are called to, whether that be as a full-time SAHM or a full-time working mom or somewhere in between, I believe you can have the rest you need and the help you desire as long as you ask for it.

For some of you, it might be hiring out help because you can't keep up with the cooking, cleaning, and housework. For others of you, it might be finding a daycare once a week so you can start on your own God-idea/business plan and you need the space to think. Remember, you may not be able to change your husband's circumstances or the fact that he is gone a lot—but you can change your perspective. You can ask God for help to withstand the hardships that come from this lifestyle. Instead of feeling helpless and burnt-out, you truly can feel filled up and fulfilled! As your priorities shift and your heart softens and you begin to seek God first in everything you do, your husband may start to reconsider all of those late hours at the office. He may start to make his own shifts in priorities where he can be home more.

As I stopped making Cody feel bad for being gone so much and complaining about our situation with anger and hurtful words, God started moving in his heart too. He became more flexible with his schedule and spending intentional time with us. He started to grow in his role as husband and father, too, and we've been able to talk about what is most important to us and how to continue to put family first, despite the lifestyle we live and the dreams that we are working towards. God always makes a way and teaches us those important lessons as we grow in Him!

****

Now, let's chat about "single mommin' it" while your husband is right there in the home. This is another huge issue that I see in marriages, and I have absolutely felt this in my own home too. Like I said earlier, men can be very unemotional creatures and have a hard time opening up. They may have no idea how their isolation and detachment is hurting you. They may be spending all of their time in the garage tinkering on a project, spending too much time at happy hour after work, or come home so depleted or stressed that he heads straight to the living room to relax. Meanwhile, you are struggling just to get by and feel like you're on your own because your husband is deciding not to be present with you. And it hurts because that's a decision that he is making willfully. He's not in tune with your needs or the fact that you want to simply do life with him, and you feel so distant that you question if it's even worth it anymore.

I want to speak to your soul for just a minute.

Your marriage is not a mistake. God did not bring the two of you together for it to fall apart. God did not create your marriage to be one-sided and for you to feel alone. Your Father in Heaven has every single piece of your story mapped out, taken care of, and He sees it all. He knows you feel a massive void in your life where you feel your husband should be. He knows you feel anger towards him not showing up better for you and your kids. He sees how hard you are working and He wants you to know how much He loves you. And He also wants you to know how much He loves your husband, too.

This is the stage where you will fight for your marriage with the power of the Holy Spirit. This is the part of your story where you will find out who you are because of who God says you are. This is the part where you will start to understand that God is the only one who can fill this void you feel so deeply. This is the part where you will have a complete identity shift and it will change everything for your marriage. This is the part where we take what is in your mind and move it into your heart. This is not just about behavior modification; this is about heart transformation!

This is the part where God will work miracles in your life because you are ready to submit everything to Him, including your marriage. This is the good part, sister!

SCRIPTURE:
James 3:16-18
"For wherever there is jealousy and selfish ambition, there you will find disorder and evil of every kind. But the wisdom from above is first of all pure. It is also peace loving, gentle at all times, and willing to yield to others. It is full of mercy and good deeds. It shows no favoritism and is always sincere. And those who are peacemakers will plant seeds of peace and reap a harvest of righteousness."

PRAYER:
Abba, I am ready. I am ready to release it all to you. I am ready to loosen this grip I have over my life and my marriage and surrender it to you. I am tired of operating like a single mom. I am tired of being angry and bitter towards my absent husband. I am ready to ask for the help that I need. Forgive me for any pride that I have been carrying around that has caused chaos, busyness, and stress to come into my home. I'm ready to find my rest in you. I'm ready to fill this void in my life with you. Open my heart fully and show me how much you love me and my husband. Show me the peace that can only come from you. I love you. Amen.

QUESTIONS:

1. Where can you ask for help in the day-to-day if you are falling into the category of "I can do it all?"
2. What cultural narrative are you believing about motherhood, marriage, or work that is contributing to the issue of feeling like a single mom and breeding resentment?
3. Think back to that hurt you felt from Chapter 4, when your husband wasn't helping you with anything. What emotion do you feel? Journal out your feelings and your hurts here.

   We'll be uncovering where that comes from in Chapter 9!

9.
Daughter of God

Connor O'Reilly was a penniless Irishman in the last century who dreamed of emigrating to America. Finally, his dream came true when a wealthy relative bought him passage on an ocean liner. Even though he had a ticket to board, O'Reilly was still worried about not being able to afford meals during the voyage. So he planned ahead and used his few shillings to buy loaves of bread, and stuffed them into his tattered suitcase. For the week he was at sea, O'Reilly would regularly sneak down into his berth and eat stale bread for his meals, while the other well-to-do passengers enjoyed the delicious fare in the ship's dining room. As others enjoyed the food, O'Reilly would stand outside, casting longing stares through the windows.

The evening before the ship was to dock in New York, a man asked O'Reilly to join him for the evening meal. "Ah, many thanks to you," said Connor. "But I don't have any money."

"What are you talking about?" the other passenger exclaimed. "Your ticket to board was also your ticket to the ship's dining room. You've had three lovely meals a day already paid for since you left home!"

Poor O'Reilly! He spent a week eating stale bread when he could have been feasting on amazing food in the company of his fellow passengers. The blessings were already there waiting for him. (Excerpt and interpretation from *The Prayer of Jabez Devotional* by Bruce Wilkinson).

Most of us probably don't like to admit it, but we have felt like Connor more often than not when it comes to our walk with God. We've felt on the outskirts, watching other people experience His blessings, abundance, and goodness and wondering what's wrong with us? We haven't felt good enough to be included into His family. We have felt like His love is reserved for everyone else, but not us. We have felt like we've messed up too many times for Him to accept us as we are and that the shame we feel is deserved. We feel like things will never change. So like O'Reilly, we hold on to the little that we have and do our best to get by.

I felt like this for most of my adult life. Wanting and desiring the love, warmth and blessings of God, but always feeling on the outside. Never feeling quite good enough for Him or that I just needed to work harder to get to the promise. And as I took a look at my own past and the things I went through, God started to show me the hard parts of my heart that needed to be healed. He revealed to me the lies I had been believing about who I am and how they had become so ingrained in my head. He showed me how these wounds I was uncovering were impacting my marriage. He took me back to the beginning so that He could bring me back home, to Him.

My parents divorced when I was a little girl. I have no memories of my mom and dad being together, as they both remarried when I was around five. I remember finding the good in the situation. Wherever there was a negative, I looked for a positive. I'm not sure how I learned that, but I know that's what I did to cope with the situation.

I lived full-time with my mom, stepdad, brother and two stepbrothers and visited my dad once a month, with longer periods over the summer. I always felt loved by my parents and knew they were doing the best they could for us, but there is a big difference between logically knowing in your brain that you are loved and taken care of versus actually feeling it in your heart.

I knew my daddy loved me, but I also cried myself to sleep a lot because I missed him. I knew my daddy loved me, but he was building a life and family with someone else and that was confusing and hard. I knew my mom and dad loved me—so I decided to keep my emotions to myself as much as possible to protect them. To not make them feel worse for what had happened. My motto was to stay focused on all the good things in my life and everything will be ok. I found the silver lining in every situation— at least that's how I appeared to be.

I'll never forget when I was in first grade, our school offered a program for kids with divorced parents. I remember feeling so special being part of this club. Once a month, we would get to have lunch in the counselor's office, away from all the noise and sticky floors of the cafeteria and the other kids. Myself and about six other kids would eat and chat with the counselor. It's hard to remember what we talked about, but I imagine we talked a lot about our feelings. The counselor gave us a safe place to gather and relate to others who could understand us. It wasn't necessarily a club you wanted to be a part of, but it did make me feel seen and special. It made me feel like everything was going to be ok, even if my parents were split up. It made me feel like I wasn't alone. Unfortunately, this was the last time I was actually open and honest about how I was really feeling about my parents' divorce and the toll that it was taking on my little heart. As I got older, I actually began to believe I was luckier than others and blessed by the fact of having divorced parents. My dad had three more children and I saw my half-siblings as a blessing. I absolutely adored them and loved spending time with them when I visited my dad. I was able to pursue basketball from the time I was in 4th grade to my sophomore year in college, and I always told myself that if my parents had never gotten divorced, maybe I would never have played basketball. My stepdad was my coach, and he and my mom were always my biggest supporters. Who was I to ever wish that away? Who am I to wish my past was different when my present is pretty dang good and my future is looking bright? Again, avoid the negative and let's just focus on the positive.

What I see now is that I was just trying to suppress all of my deepest emotions. In my mind, it would have been unkind of me to share with my mom how much I missed my dad because she was working her tail off to give me a great life, filled with love and support and I did not want to make her feel bad for something we could not change. It would have made my dad feel guilty if I had told him that the family pictures excluding me and my brother, the vacations they took without us, and the way that I felt in his home made me feel like an outcast. I worked so hard to try and shove down this feeling of being an outsider and instead look at everything through rose colored glasses. I even did a presentation in my senior year Humanities class about my parents' divorce being one of the best things that ever happened to me. A blessing in disguise, I called it. And I remember presenting it to my class with a huge knot in my throat, holding back the tears. But they weren't tears of joy. They were tears of heartbreak that I would not let myself actually feel. It was a presentation of something that I thought I "should" say, not something that I actually believed.

On the outside, I was this successful student athlete with lots of friends and opportunities. I was invited to the parties and probably considered one of the "popular" girls. I was nominated for Homecoming court, celebrated 1,000 career points and broke scoring records during my high school basketball career, and was on the National Honor Society. I did my best to be happy, find success in everything, and do what was expected of me. No one, and I mean no one, would have pegged me as someone struggling internally. Heck, I did such a good job of suppressing my deepest emotions that I was fooling myself too. My identity was wrapped up into all of the things that I did, and it seemed like I was doing everything just fine, thank you very much. But those wounds and those suppressed hurts from my childhood were getting ready to catch up to me, whether I wanted them to or not.

When I met Cody before my senior year of college, I felt truly seen and accepted by him in a way I had never felt before. It was almost like he was able to identify that I had been acting out my part in this play called life and somehow he was able to get me to take the mask off. Somehow I felt like the *real* Shayla with him, instead of the Shayla that everyone else wanted me to be. When I was with Cody, I felt free to be me. There was no pretending with him. There were no appearances to keep up. There was nothing I had to do to earn his love; he just freely gave it. It was a kind of love that was so pure and so real and I knew I was going to marry this boy. No other love could compare to what I felt with him. He saw me, accepted me, and loved me.

After graduation, I couldn't pack my bags fast enough to leave my old life behind and start a new one with Cody. But in those bags, I packed more than just my clothes and toothbrush. I packed my people pleasing side. I packed my need for worldly validation. I packed my deepest hurts and wounds. I packed the need to be accepted, perfect, and successful. I packed my old self into those bags and brought it with me because I figured that Cody was my prince charming. Surely he would be able to fix me and fill those voids I had been feeling in my heart for so long. His love was enough to keep me going, moving me forward in life. I finally found my husband, so cowboy please take me away!

What I didn't see then was that I was expecting Cody to save me. I wanted to run from a life of divorce and brokenness. I wanted to run from a past of people pleasing. I wanted him to protect me from people in my past who had truly hurt me, making me feel like I wasn't welcome, loved, or worth anything. With Cody, it felt like I had a fresh start and I didn't have to deal with all of that junk anymore.

However, when you expect another human being to love you perfectly or to heal you and take away your hurts, you are setting yourself up for failure. Another person, not even your husband, was meant to fill those shoes. But this is exactly what the world wants us to think. Why else do fairytales end at the wedding? Because they don't want to show the actual hard parts of marriage. The hero gets the girl and it's happily ever after, right? Why are there songs talking about your spouse completing you, saving you, and giving you everything you need?

10 Things I Hate About My Husband

Everything about marriage is romanticized to the point where we truly believe another person on this earth can fill us with everything we need. So, we expect it. We demand it. As little girls, we dream of it. And when we aren't happy and getting our needs met—we immediately go to doomsday with our marriage. *Maybe I made the wrong choice? Maybe someone else would love me better? Why are we fighting all of the time? Is this what I signed up for?* And on and on, the lies continue to stack up, the hurtful words continue to be spoken, and the unresolved wounds continue to fester. Until one day, you are looking at yourself in the mirror wondering who the heck you are, why you are so unhappy, and why your marriage seems to be falling apart at the seams!

Sister, I've been there. I had very Cinderella-esque experiences growing up, where I felt like I wasn't wanted. That made me believe I had to work to be loved. These thoughts placed me in the shadows, where I felt like I belonged. Until one day, my prince charming showed up. And just as Cinderella was frisked away to her happily ever after, I believed Cody was my everything and I had a fresh start. Our wedding and the beginning of our marriage screamed perfection—but real life isn't a fairytale. Real life doesn't end at the wedding. And not only were my childhood wounds starting to affect my marriage and how I treated my husband, they were also impacting my identity. They affected my view of God and who He really is to me. They made me feel like an orphan removed from His love.

It's time we unpack the bag once and for all. It's time we take those old pants and shirts and drop them off at Helping Hands because they don't fit any more. It's time we face our wounds and our hurts so we can understand exactly how they've shown up in our marriage and in our life. It's time we allow the one true Healer to dispose of all the junk not serving us anymore, so that we can be set completely free.

December 2022 was a turning point in my life, and what became the blueprint for the book you are holding in your hands.

My life was good and it felt like my marriage had gotten stronger, but I still wasn't satisfied. My business was going well, but I wasn't where I wanted to be. Outside of those things, it was like God was calling me to take a look at my heart for the first time and I finally felt ready. I knew this inner work was going to be hard and uncomfortable, but I knew it was the only way to get where God was calling me to go.

Through a recommendation from a friend, I hired Heather as my coach. She's a Christian business coach specializing in mindset, heart-set, and soul-care. I didn't even "shop around" for another coach. She was immediately the one that I felt could help me unlock the next version of me. And that is exactly what happened. Through her guidance and support, she began to help me see God's true character and the pieces in my past that God was wanting to heal. She identified an orphan spirit in me that was holding me back from experiencing true freedom in Christ and where and how that spirit had taken root in my life. In a profound way, the Holy Spirit met us during every call and I was able to start to see myself the way that God sees me—as His loved and chosen daughter. Over the next few months, He poured out His love on me in ways I had never felt before.

> I started to see why I was playing small in my business and felt unworthy of success and had made it an idol.

> I started to see where I had been hurt in my past, and how I let toxic positivity control my life for a very long time.

> I started to see how the devil used guilt and shame to taunt me and keep me stuck.

> I started to see where God actually wanted to take me and who He says I am.

10 Things I Hate About My Husband

I started to understand that His promises are yes and amen for me too!

One wound at a time, God began to do His healing work in my heart that allowed His love to take residence so that everything else that wasn't Him was pushed out. He helped me to forgive those I needed to forgive, let go of the lies and identities that I had deemed to be true, and look forward to a future filled with Him as my constant.

God began speaking to me strongly through dreams, songs, shows, and people. Some people might call them "coincidences" but there are no coincidences when it comes to God and the messages He has for us. For example, when my son Leroy was obsessed with the movie Frozen, the character Elsa and the song "Let it Go" for a full month, God used that time to remind me that the old me was gone, that my fears don't control me anymore, and that I don't have to be perfect for Him. He loves me just as I am and I am free in Him. He used the TV show "1883" to give me a visual of His Father's love for me. Elsa (yeah, I know, ironic right?), the teenage daughter in the show, was the apple of her Daddy's eye and when she was fatally shot with a bow and arrow at the end of the show and nearing the end of her life, her dad let her choose where she wanted to be buried and that was where the family would spend the rest of their days, too. As Elsa and her dad, James, took off on horseback, with this beautiful picture of a Daddy holding his daughter and riding off into the sunset, I could feel God say to me, "That's what I would do for you. I would go to the ends of the earth for you. I will never let you go."

And as the last scene unfolded, with James holding Elsa in his arms as she took her last breath, leaning up against a big oak tree, I wept. I wept because even though my earthly father may not have perfectly portrayed this kind of love, God does. I wept because I no longer felt like I had anything to prove to earn God's love. It was free. I wept because I was no longer an orphan and I truly felt like God's daughter, not just in my mind but in my heart. There was nothing that I had to do to receive His love. I only had to accept it.

A month later, I was at a leadership event in Louisiana and was having a prayer morning with two of my friends. I was relaying the events of these two experiences and how I felt God spoke to me and how ironic it was that He used the name Elsa twice to speak to me. My friend Rebecca immediately did a search on Google and said, "Oh my word. Elsa means 'consecrated to God.' It means 'God is my oath.' There is no doubt that God was speaking to you and bringing you closer to Him." I mean c'mon, just go ahead and hand me those tissues again, please! I am consecrated, dedicated, and belong to God. He is my Father and my everything. And the same goes for you.

The scripture that perfectly sums up our identity as children of God is Romans 8:14-17: "*The mature children of God are those who are moved by the impulses of the Holy Spirit. And you did not receive the "spirit of religious duty," leading you back into the fear of never being good enough. But you have received the "spirit of full acceptance," enfolding you into the family of God. And you will never feel orphaned, for as he rises up within us, our spirits join him in saying the words of tender affection, "Beloved Father!" For the Holy Spirit makes God's fatherhood real to us as he whispers into our innermost being, "You are God's beloved Child!" And since we are his true children, we qualify to share all his treasures, for indeed, we are heirs of God himself. And since we are joined to Christ, we also inherit all that he is and all that he has. We will experience being co-glorified with him provided that we accept his sufferings as our own.*"

Something happened to me because of God's love and kindness—my heart changed. It softened. He brought me back into His house and lavished His love on me. Despite my failings, my sins, my past and my own issues, He welcomed me back, as His daughter, and nothing will ever change that.

10 Things I Hate About My Husband

Romans 8:38: "*And I am convinced that nothing can ever separate us from God's love. Neither death nor life, neither angels nor demons, neither our fears for today nor our worries about tomorrow-not even the powers of hell can separate us from God's love.*"

I can't mention this kind of love from a father to his child, without thinking of the prodigal son story. In Luke 15:11-32, Jesus shares the parable of the lost son. He asks his father for his inheritance and his father freely gives it. And the son goes out and squanders it on parties, booze, and wild living. And as he reaches the very end of himself, broke, alone and hungrier than even the pigs he is feeding, he comes to his senses and heads back home. With his tail between his legs, he is prepared to beg his father for forgiveness. He is prepared to work for his father as a slave because he believes he is no longer worthy of being his son after the stunt he pulled. But lo and behold in verse 20 we read, "*So he returned home to his father. And while he was still a long way off, his father saw him coming. Filled with love and compassion, he ran to his son, embraced him, and kissed him.*" The father showered him with a robe, a ring, sandals, and a feast to celebrate that he is home again! Regardless of what he had done, he was still his son and was welcomed home with open arms. His father had spent all of his time just waiting for this moment. This is the picture of who God is to us. No matter how far we stray, we are still His children and He is just waiting for us to come back home to Him.

At first, I was honestly flabbergasted that I identified as having an orphan spirit. I have been a Christian my entire life. I had been reading my Bible. I had been going to church. I had been reading devotionals. I thought I knew Jesus. This can't be a thing, can it? But in my heart, I hadn't felt His overwhelming and transformative love. I hadn't felt like a true daughter. The orphan spirit had taken root from my past experiences and childhood and the devil was doing everything he could to make sure I held on to it. Because if he can trick you into feeling like an orphan, not feeling good enough for God, then he can trap you. You will continue to live in a cycle of false freedom, a cycle of shame and guilt, believing all of his lies, not being able to share your own story of God's redemption with others.

I could go on and on about the orphan spirit. How it originated in the Garden of Eden when God's perfect home was destroyed by the tempter and Adam and Eve had to leave. What it means to be adopted by God and what His true nature is. And how every single thing in your life will change once you realize your true identity as a daughter of God… but I don't have enough space to include every single thing. To dig deeper and for more information, I recommend checking out Leif Hetland's book, *Healing the Orphan Spirit*. His book taught me so much and was a huge catalyst in my own journey towards freedom in Christ. Leif is the founder and president of Global Mission Awareness, author of numerous books, and a ministry leader teaching on God's Kingdom Family. The same freedom that became available to me is available to you!

Just like me, you may have some neglect and abandonment issues you've never dealt with. You've been hurt, betrayed, or felt alone. There is no trauma, big or small, that the devil cannot grab a hold of and use against you to keep you stuck. Don't be fooled or "toxic positivity" your way out of recognizing the pain from your past that is keeping you from experiencing God's magnificent, Fatherly love. Going deeper with God and allowing Him to heal the hard parts in your heart is exactly what will set you free from the bondage of an orphan spirit and an enemy who wants to keep causing strife and division in your life. (*See the prayer at the back of this book to help you with healing your orphan spirit.*)

Maybe you've never felt a father's love like the one Elsa had in real life. And maybe, like me, you've brought those heart wounds to the marriage, not realizing that you were putting the expectation on your husband to heal it. You didn't realize until now, that when your husband ignored your need for words of affirmation, that it was puncturing another hole in your already hurting heart. A hurting heart that was trying to forget the hateful, demeaning, and harmful words spoken over you your entire life. You didn't realize until now that when your husband is absent all the time and you respond with anger, that it's the pain of rejection pouring out of you. You didn't realize until now that you've been wanting your husband to be more and do more and be your knight in shining armor because you are bound and determined to not repeat a history that you want to forget.

Here is the truth: Your husband cannot be your Holy Spirit. Your husband is an imperfect human and is not your savior. Jesus is. And what He wants to show you is that when you receive His love and live from that place of intimacy, you honestly won't need anything else. When you get your value, love, purpose and affirmation from Christ, you won't look to your husband for it. Who does the Bible say is your refuge- God or your husband? *"The eternal God is your refuge, and his everlasting arms are under you."* Deuteronomy 33:27 (NLT)

Whether you have meant to or not, you've turned your husband and your marriage into an idol by believing he can fulfill all of your needs. I love what Gary Thomas writes in his book *Loving Him Well*: "Just as surely as a block of wood can't speak wisdom, so a human man can't love you as God created you to be loved. And what happens when an idol disappoints you? Bitterness, sadness, and sometimes even despair." And oh, do I know that to be true! When my husband wasn't loving me the way that I thought I needed, bitterness, sadness and despair followed and the enemy's lies got louder and louder, drowning out God's voice and love.

My approach to transform my marriage was that I was more focused on falling in love with Jesus instead of falling in love with my husband. God was my need; my husband was a want. He was a bonus. And as we will talk about in the next chapter, your relationship with God has the potential to transform your husband in ways that you've only ever dreamed about!

As Holy Spirit took residence in my heart and I truly felt like the daughter of God that I was created to be, I began to see like God sees. I began to see my husband the way that God sees him. As loved and cherished and adored. I even developed compassion and grace for his shortcomings. I felt unconditional love. I knew that we would be ok because I now had the One who was meant to fulfill me all along.

We all have a story. We all have a past. But I'm here to say that when you let God heal your past and you find your identity in Him and only Him, He can make all things new. Including your marriage!

SCRIPTURE:

Ephesians 3:17-21 (NLT)

"Then, by constantly using your faith, the life of Christ will be released deep inside you, and the resting place of his love will become the very source and root of your life. Then you will be empowered to discover what every holy one experiences- the great magnitude of the astonishing love of Christ in all its dimensions. How deeply intimate and far-reaching is his love! How enduring and inclusive it is! Endless love beyond measurement that transcends our understanding- this extravagant love pours into you until you are filled to overflowing with the fullness of God! Never doubt God's mighty power to work in you and accomplish all this. He will achieve infinitely more than your greatest request, your most unbelievable dream, and exceed your wildest imagination! He will outdo them all, for his miraculous power constantly energizes you. Now we offer up to God all the glorious praise that rises from every church in every generation through Jesus Christ- and all that will yet be manifest through time and eternity. Amen!"

10 Things I Hate About My Husband

PRAYER:

Father God, your love is raining down on me right now. I am so overwhelmed at the vastness of it. How wide, how long, how high, and how deep your love is for me and my husband. Thank you for the gift of your precious son, Jesus, who you sent to die for my sins. I now understand how much you love me and what that sacrifice actually means. I declare that I am a daughter of God and no longer an orphan. I once was lost but now I am found. Thank you for never leaving me. I pray that this walk we are on together will continue to get deeper and deeper and deeper. I love you Abba. Amen.

QUESTIONS:

1. As you read this chapter, what heart wounds or painful circumstances came up for you? Don't label it as not important or not as big as someone else's. Your trauma and pain is specific to you and only you. How is that pain creeping into your marriage? Use this time to connect the dots between your past and your current circumstances.

2. In what ways is being a daughter difficult? When you think of God's love being freely given to you, how do you respond to that? Dig deeper to see what walls are up or what lies you are believing as to why you can't experience God's love.

3. Forgiveness leads to love. Who is on your heart to forgive? This is not about placing blame on anyone, but about setting yourself free from a past that you cannot change. Whether people in your past hurt you on purpose or they unknowingly hurt you, it's best to bring it to God and ask Him to give you the strength to forgive. We live in a fallen world, with a very real enemy who wants you to hold on to the hurt. But God says in John 16:33: "*I have told you all this so that you may have peace in me. Here on earth, you will have many trials and sorrows. But take heart because I have overcome the world.*" (NLT)

4. In what ways have you made your husband or marriage an idol?

10.
But He Just Doesn't Get It

In March of 2023, God gave me a dream to write a book about marriage. The book you are holding in your hand. He downloaded all of it. He gave me the title, the chapters, and the foundation of how my marriage has grown and His part in the restoration. In complete obedience, I immediately started working on it, and as the months went by, added more and more of what God was teaching me and healing in me. I kept it a secret at first, but knew eventually, this was going to need to be shared.

As someone who has been working in the on-line, social media space for years now, I decided to take to TikTok with the message God was giving me to share. I love doing videos and providing value, but I just wasn't quite sure where to start. *Is anyone else talking about seeking God first to transform their marriage? Is anyone else talking about what to do if you are really struggling with bitterness and resentment towards your husband?* I was curious and wanted to see what else was out there. So, I did a little market research.

I did a simple search of "Godly marriage" on TikTok. And you know what mostly came up in my results? Men, Godly men, speaking to other men about how to lead their wives and how to pursue God fervently to bring that back to the family. No joke—all the videos I found were men. And on one hand, that is great because we desperately need Godly men to help others rise up and become the man of God they were created to be. On the other hand, where are the women who are speaking to other women who do not have a husband that believes in God?

As I watched these videos, I immediately thought of the

woman whose husband is not the spiritual leader of their home. Whose husband is not at all tuning in to listen to those TikTok videos. God gave me a vision of that woman watching these videos of Godly men and I could feel her pain and sadness from the harsh reality and disappointment to know that she isn't blessed with a man like that… one who takes care of her, leads her, goes to church with her and prays with her. God really pressed it upon my heart to make my first video for her; to let her know she isn't alone and that there is hope for her marriage. I wanted her to know that she does have the power to influence her husband and that I was going to be talking about this issue on my profile.

The comments and views came flooding in:
- "This!!! Followed so fast."
- "Instant follow. Please send help."
- "What a blessing to come across your page. Thank you!"
- "That's exactly what I'm going through now!"

Hundreds of comments and over 100,000 views later, I felt like I had my confirmation that this is exactly what God was calling me to speak about. I don't tell you these numbers to brag or boast, but to share that this is a real need many women have and relate to. So many women are clearly yearning for a Godly man and they feel so stuck in their marriages.

Many think that if their husband would just change, that would solve all their problems. Some think that there is someone else out there that would be better for them. Some are worried that their husband will never change and they'll just keep growing further and further apart. I've even seen women scared to pursue God more because they are worried their husband will leave them! If any of this resonates with you, then I know you will appreciate my story of how my own transformation became a catalyst for my husband's as well.

I was the kind of wife who would watch videos of pastors preaching to the husbands about marriage and I would send them to Cody. I would let him know that this is what *he* needed to be doing to make our marriage better. I thought to myself *I'm square with God, but since I'm not totally sure where you stand, you need to listen to this.* My intentions were good, but my heart posture screamed "you're the problem."

When I sent him those videos, I was reminding him of his flaws. I was **pushing** God on him instead of inviting Him in. Reminding him once again that I was always right and he was the one who needed to change. I wanted him to be the one to save me and fulfill me; I just figured he needed some direction to get him to see what I needed… to try and create a freedom in my life that Cody wasn't capable of giving me. But, of course, it did nothing to save my marriage and only pushed him away more. It was not an act of grace, mercy or love because it was motivated by my own selfish wants.

As God began healing my heart and I got to know Him on a much deeper level, he taught me that it wasn't my job to save my husband. Actually, it's not my job to save anyone. My one and only job is to pursue Him. Seek Him. Receive His love. And He told me that as He transforms my heart and life, He'll take care of my husband. Just like Cody can't be my Holy Spirit, neither can I be his. And when we push instead of influence, all we're doing is creating more division. When we **push** instead of **pray**, we are acting as God instead of trusting God to take care of the situation.

The more I thought about it, the more I realized that my pushing and nagging only made my husband feel like something was wrong with him. It made him feel like he was less than me. It made him feel pressured to change. What I saw as growth, he was seeing as more work and being uncomfortable. It was new to him and it was personal to him and he just really wanted me to leave him alone.

We can get so caught up in our own agendas and our own

needs and wants, that we forget to trust the very One who takes care of us. We so badly want our husband to have a relationship with God like we have (especially because we think it will make our own lives better), but we forget that no one pushed us into it. We forget that we had our own moment with Him and we are all on our own journeys. *You cannot be responsible for a realization that you haven't had yet or that your husband hasn't had yet.* Remember when you were full of sin, wandering and lost, not knowing your true identity—was it an act of love that brought you to Christ or was it an act of pushing?

It is God who makes our hearts ready to receive Him and our eyes are opened to the freedom He has planned for us. Another human being is not responsible for the shift and internal spiritual hunger for God that we have experienced... God is. The truth is that God doesn't need anyone to accomplish His purposes for Him. He chooses to use others to influence in a less demanding way.

There are more than enough examples in the Bible of the powerful ways in which God used women for his purposes and glory, despite the time period being less than accommodating towards women. I mean, Jesus came into this world through a woman. Not a single male had anything to do with the conception or birth of our Lord. Mary is the only one who contributed to Jesus' DNA! What about the prostitute who entered the home of the Pharisee, who was eating with Jesus. The Pharisee was appalled that she was kneeling at Jesus' feet, washing them with her tears and perfume. But Jesus praised her in front of the man saying *"I tell you, her sins-and they are many-have been forgiven, so she has shown me much love. But a person who has forgiven little shows only little love."* (Luke 7:47 NLT). Verse 50 goes on to say: *"And Jesus said to the woman, 'Your faith has saved you; go in peace.'"*

The Bible highlights that women were present during Christ's crucifixion in Mark 15:40-41 and women were the ones present to give testimony of the greatest event in our world's history, when Jesus rose from the dead! In the book, *Loving Him*

Shayla Huber

Well Gary Thomas highlights the importance and power of women by saying "The Bible presents a woman as a strong image bearer of God, able to stand against the world, powerfully influencing men and culture (witness Deborah in the Bible or Teresa of Avila in history) as she lives the life God created her to live." It truly blows my mind that even in such a male-oriented culture in which the Bible took shape, God was elevating, nurturing, and setting apart women to be change-agents for their families and for the world. And He has the same goal in mind for you!

I never used to hold my head high as a woman of God. Shame always reared its ugly head every time I yelled, acted in anger, or said something hurtful. I would think that a true woman of God doesn't do that. She is gentle, quiet, patient, and submissive, and well, I was the furthest thing from submissive. I was also the furthest thing from patient and quiet. The guilt ate at me because even when I tried to be more patient and I, once again, messed up, it felt like I was never going to get it right. I was never going to be the "good Christian wife" that so many women try to live up to. You know, the infamous Proverbs 31 woman.

I adopted the identity, and even had people speak over me, that I am just an angry person. I do get fired up and passionate about things. Maybe it was this red hair I was born with and inherited from my own, very passionate and outspoken Grandfather. It always felt like such a negative thing. I was able to channel a lot of passion into my work, but at home, it was always something negative. If you have ever felt like you can't seem to get it right when it comes to being a submissive, meek, and quiet wife and it is something that you've believed you needed to become in order to be a better wife, let me enlighten you for a moment.

The word "meek" in Greek means "praus." The definition is gentle, mild, meek or regulated anger, tame, or subdued. This was a Greek military term that they used when taming wild horses to be used in battle. They would take this wild horse, full of strength, power, and anger and they would break them to ride, work, march, and fight. They specifically chose the most intense wild horses because they knew that once they "meekened" them, under the will of their master, they would be able to point their power and strength in the right direction. For a purpose. They did not take away the sheer power of the horse—they controlled it.

Matthew 5:5 says: *"Blessed are the meek (humble), for they shall inherit the earth."* And Titus 3:2 says: *"They must not slander anyone and must avoid quarreling. Instead, they should be gentle and show true humility to everyone."* Finally, as it pertains to wives, 1 Peter 3:4 tells us: *"You should clothe yourselves instead with the beauty that comes from within, the unfading beauty of a gentle and quiet spirit, which is so precious to God."*

Ladies, if we are called to be meek and submissive, then it is absolutely crucial that you understand what that actually means! It does not mean that we need to become a doormat, have no opinions, and try to change some of the personality traits that God gave us that make us unique. It means first and foremost submitting to our master (God), so that He can take our power and our strength and even our anger and channel it in the way that it should go! Being a meek woman is not a negative in God's eyes. It means that you are still very powerful and strong, but you are able to use it for the will of God.

Being a meek woman means that you are strong, you are self-controlled, and you are absolutely needed for battle. You have a purpose when it comes to influencing your husband, your role as a wife and mother, and your Kingdom assignment. The world may have given you the impression that being a meek woman makes you less than or that you don't have a voice or that you need to be walked all over. Oh no, my friend, quite the opposite. Being meek means you're a war horse, ready for battle, and you know how to submit to your master so that He can help you take that wildness inside of you and use it to move mountains for the kingdom of God!

My husband did not marry a quiet and submissive wife, and

I know that he loves the ambitions and the drive that God gave me. But I struggled letting him lead. I struggled with anger and holding my tongue. As God healed my heart and started transforming me into my true identity as a daughter of His, he meekened me. He helped me become more gentle, patient and meek, not because I was less than my husband, but because He knew the strength and power He gave me would ultimately help my husband in his own walk with God and restore our rightful roles as husband and wife. God took me, this wild and out of control horse, and he meekened me so that the fruits of the Spirit, instead of having to force them, would naturally flow out of me. The impartation that I experienced through God's love was released to my husband and it truly changed everything for us.

Your pursuit of Christ and the actions that follow will be something that does get noticed by your husband. The internal and external changes that he sees in you will get his attention. Your tone of voice being filled with grace instead of harshness after he forgets to take out the trash, your servant heart that chooses to spend time with him over finishing a work project that can wait, your peace and joy cooking supper and the light that seems to be shining through you as you dance with your kids in the kitchen— he will notice.

As you seek God first in everything and He begins to do His healing work inside of your heart, His love will flow out of you. Instead of my heart posture begging for my husband to know God more to benefit me, it has been for Cody to experience the overwhelming and overflowing love of God in his own life. God has shown me over and over that it isn't my job. It's His job. And the more Cody sees me on the couch with my Bible and he sees the impact I'm making in other's lives by sharing my own story— the more we talk about it. I am able to share things with him that I never had the courage to say before because now it's coming from a place of identity and love, instead of striving to know the Lord with an orphan heart or striving to mold my husband into what I wanted him to be.

10 Things I Hate About My Husband

Genesis 2:24 says: *"Therefore a man shall leave his father and his mother and hold fast to his wife, and they shall become one flesh."* (NLT) When you become married, you become one. I love the promise of this scripture and I believe this is what God has designed for us. But your "oneness" does not mean you are always on the exact same page in your walk with the Lord. That does not mean that you walk at the same pace or think the same thoughts or pursue the same things at the same time. Just like you have your own heart wounds and stuff to work through—so does your husband. Beneath the anger that he displays, his vices, or his withdrawals, is a pain that he is avoiding. Pain that only God can heal.

If you believe in the promise of becoming one, then you must trust the Lord to accomplish that. You must trust the Lord with your husband. Let the Holy Spirit shine in you and through you. God did not design women to just be passive victims in marriage, rather we are active participants for His glory. Remember...we are meek, we are not helpless! We are made in His image and have so much power through the Holy Spirit to influence our husbands. God is specific and detailed and the scripture below perfectly describes the authority we have been given in Jesus Christ!

Here we are in John 14 with Jesus comforting the disciples before the crucifixion. Jesus is preparing to leave them and they are freaking out because if Jesus leaves them, how will they know where to go? They were operating as orphans and were fearful of Jesus not being in their presence. Jesus is preparing to share with them that He is the only way to God because he is both God and man. By uniting our lives with His, we are united with God. Read this scripture and pay attention to the power that is being released through Jesus Christ.

John 14:5-14: *Thomas said to him, "Master, we don't know where you're going, so how could we know the way there?"*

Jesus explained, "I am the Way, I am the Truth, and I am the Life. No one comes next to the Father except through union with me. To know me is to know my Father too. And from now on you will realize that you have seen him and experienced him."

Phillip spoke up, "Lord, show us the Father, and that will be all that we need!"

Jesus replied, "Phillip, I've been with you all this time and you still don't know who I am? How could you ask me to show you the Father, for anyone who has looked at me has seen the Father. Don't you believe that the Father is living in me and that I am living in the Father? Even my words are not my own but come from my Father, he lives in me and performs his miracles of power through me. Believe that I live as one with my Father and that my Father lives as one with me- or at least, believe because of the mighty miracles I have done. I tell you this timeless truth: The person who follows me in faith, believing in me, will do the same mighty miracles that I do- even greater miracles than these because I go to be with my Father! For I will do whatever you ask me to do when you ask me in my name. And that is how the Son will show what the Father is really like and bring glory to him. Ask me anything in my name, and I will do it for you!"

Do you see it? Jesus had to die on the cross for our sins, and because He came back to life and then ascended to heaven; He released the Holy Spirit to us! He gave us power through the blood of Jesus Christ! Father, Son, and Holy Spirit is the very family nature that God is trying to teach the world. God loves us that much that He would sacrifice His son for us and then give us the ability to declare miracles, in the name of Jesus! Jesus couldn't stay here on earth and give us the Holy Spirit. He had to ascend to Heaven to accomplish this. And through the power of his mighty name, we are given authority!

Acts 1:6-8 confirms our authority by saying: *"So when the apostles were with Jesus, they kept asking him, 'Lord, has the time come for you to free Israel and restore our kingdom?' He replied, 'The Father alone has the authority to set those dates and times, and they are not for you to know. But you will receive power when the Holy Spirit comes upon you. And you will be my witnesses, telling people about me everywhere- in Jerusalem, throughout Judea, in Samaria, and to the ends of the earth."* (NLT)

Again, we see in Ezekiel 36:26-28, God was promising the new covenant would ultimately be fulfilled in Christ and we would be given the opportunity to be made new and have His spirit fill us. *"And I will give you a new heart, and I will put a new spirit in you. I will take out your stony, stubborn heart and give you a tender, responsive heart. And I will put my Spirit in you so that you will follow my decrees and be careful to obey my regulations."* (NLT)

Once again, God is showing us His beautiful and glorious plan to draw His children back to Himself. To give us what we need to live a blessed life here on earth. To overwhelm us with His love and that His will for our lives is always better than what we could come up with on our own. And that He is always with us through the power of the Holy Spirit! He most definitely took out my stony and stubborn heart and replaced it with a tender and responsive heart. He meekened me so that He could restore my marriage and bring me true joy, peace and happiness. He took my anger and bitterness and turned it to love and only through the power of Jesus Christ was that possible. I've been witness to marriages restored after years of drug addiction. I've seen marriages restored after infidelity. What makes you think He can't do the same for you?

The world is going to tell you to give up. Your husband is too far gone. He's messed up too many times. Someone else out there is going to treat you better. Someone else out there is going to understand you better. You are worth more. Divorce is a way out. But the kingdom says: *"Ask me anything in my name, and I will do it for you!"* John 14:14 (NLT)

I don't know your specific situation. I don't know what you

are going through. But I do know if you continue to seek God first, rest in your identity as a daughter of God, and truly trust Him with everything—anything can happen. I believe you can have a fulfilling and incredible marriage even if your husband hasn't caught up with you in faith just yet. Don't stay hyper-focused on that, instead give it to God and stay focused on the things you do love about your husband. Be more like Jesus in the relationship and instead of judging him, serve him. Instead of being worried about him, trust that God has a plan for him.

Hoping and wishing is not enough to move and influence your husband. Pushing him and nagging him is not the answer to helping your husband know God more. Trying to change him on your own will only prolong the miracle that God wants to give you. Knowing your identity as a daughter of God, receiving the love and sacrifice that Jesus paid on the cross for us, and embracing the power of the Holy Spirit living inside of you—now that is a recipe for success!

A few months ago, I bought Cody a new Bible and a few devotionals and set them on his nightstand. Without pushing and asking, I simply made available what has brought me so much peace and joy and that when the time is right for him, he can decide to go deeper with God too. And after only a couple of weeks of me praying for him to have the desire to read that Bible, he opened it and has been learning more about God's heart ever since!

When you know **who** you are and **whose** you are, there is a Holy Confidence in that. There is a trust that you now have with God to truly take care of every single need in your life, including the desire to have a Godly and beautiful marriage and for your husband to develop that relationship with God in order to lead you better, lead your children better, and fulfill God's calling on his life too. As you push forward on your journey, remember to think of the long term benefits of interceding on behalf of your husband. Think of the legacy and wisdom you can pass down to your own children as you continue growing in Christ, instead of staying where you are and accepting less than God's best for you. There is so much fruit for you and your family on the other side of this challenge and I know God's blessings will overflow as you become the woman of God he designed you to be! God wastes nothing and I encourage you to allow God to take over this story because I have no doubt it will be used to further His kingdom!

SCRIPTURE:
1 Peter 3:1-4 (NLT)
"And now let me speak to the wives. Be devoted to your own husbands, so that even if some of them do not obey the Word of God, your kind conduct may win them over without you saying a thing. For when they observe your pure, godly life before God, it will impact them deeply. Let your true beauty come from your inner personality, not a focus on the external. For lasting beauty comes from a gentle and peaceful spirit, which is precious in God's sight and is much more important than the outward adornment of elaborate hair, jewelry, and fine clothes."

PRAYER:
Father, this prayer is for my husband today. Forgive me for doubting him. Forgive me for not treating him as you would treat him. Forgive me for doubting the authority and power that you have to do miracles in his life. I love my husband so much and want him to know you the way that I know you. And I'm declaring today that, even when I can't see it, you are working in him. Help him to see how much you love him today. Give him the desire to get to know you more. I'm chasing you Father. I'm seeking you. I love you and I can't wait to see all the beautiful things you have planned for our story. In your precious son's name, Jesus Christ. Amen.

QUESTIONS:

1. Were you surprised to learn about the real meaning of the word "meek?" How does it encourage and empower you to keep interceding on behalf of your husband?

2. In what areas of your relationship are you committed to stop pushing and instead start praying over your husband?

3. Write out your own prayer for your husband and offer him fully to God. You can be confident that as you take your focus off your husband's flaws and weaknesses, that placing him in God's hands is the safest place for him to be.

11.
M-I-L Issues

Ever had that thought that maybe the problem really isn't you, but it's the woman who raised your husband that is to blame for all of his problems? Your husband doesn't help with the housework enough because his mom didn't teach him how to run a vacuum. Your husband is closed off emotionally because his mom didn't teach him about feelings. Your husband isn't invested in your family enough because he is still putting his mommy and daddy first instead of you and your kids. Maybe the fact that she's a better cook than you even creates some tension at family gatherings! You feel that sense of "one-upness."

Whatever the case may be, if you haven't had at least one issue with your mother-in-law (MIL), then this chapter most definitely won't be for you. But I highly doubt that's the case. Attempting to place blame on someone else for our husband's shortcomings is one of the ways we try to pick the "get out of jail free card" when it comes to our marriages. Attempting to blame an outsider for issues between us and our husbands is the easy way out, instead of looking internally at the root of the problem. And as we've discussed that no husband is perfect throughout this book, I'm here to remind you that no mother-in-law is perfect, either. Let's shed some light on this super sensitive and most likely frustrating topic taking place in your life right now by first looking at what the Bible says about family after marriage.

Genesis 2:24 says: *"Therefore a man shall leave his father and mother and hold fast to his wife, and the two shall become one flesh."* (NLT) So naturally, when we get married, us ladies are ready for that transition. We are ready to have our own life, our own family, and our own space. We take our husbands by the hand, head for our new home, and say "see ya" to the in-laws. Or, like me, subconsciously you are beyond ready to leave your past behind and start a new life with the man who you believe has all the answers.

There is a romantic element to it when we think it will just be "the two of us" and that it's us against the world. (Cue song "Just the Two of Us.") But what we tend to overlook and forget is that the man you married was someone's baby boy, too. Someone else loved him and raised him before you came along.

The dynamic of the Mother-Son relationship can be complex and not easily severed. When you walked down the aisle to marry her son, your MIL was most likely overcome with happiness for the two of you, but she was probably also a little sad because life as she knew it was never going to be the same. While you saw your handsome man standing at the altar waiting for you, she was seeing her sweet little boy. (As a mother of two boys, I'm already in tears thinking about it)! And as life begins as a married couple, there is a lot to learn not only about your husband but about the woman who raised him and the expectations and boundaries that everyone has set in their own minds.

I'll never forget the first time I openly displayed my frustrations with my MIL. We were at a rodeo (we used to travel with my in-laws because Cody's dad was still competing), and my MIL, Jackie, went to grab Cody's checkbook from the truck. We had only been married a few months, and the sound of someone saying my new last name still felt weird to me. As I watched her start walking towards the arena with his checkbook in hand, I asked, "What are you doing?" She said that she was going to go pay his fees and then balance his checkbook for him.

I lost it. My face went beet red and my body temperature rose about 20 degrees. *Doesn't she realize we are married now? Isn't it my job to balance his checkbook? Why is she invading our finances? Isn't this part of the separation that is supposed to occur after the wedding?* I stormed into the trailer and shared my frustrations with Cody, complete with arms flailing and words slicing the air. I'm sure I looked like a toddler throwing a tantrum and Cody didn't quite know what to do with me.

I was supposed to be first in his life now and our finances were between the two of us. I didn't like any blurred lines. It needed to be clear cut. I was either first or I was last. Now, I do have to give myself some grace here. This was a season in our life when we were always with his parents. I'm talking every single day. Driving in the truck, sleeping in the horse trailer, eating together, literally everything. And I don't know if you know this, but a horse trailer is a very small, compact living space. There is not much privacy or room to breathe. And sometimes when I am around people for too long and crammed into such a small space for extended periods of time, I get a little cranky. I can only handle so much and had reached my limit that day.

What I did not understand was that paying Cody's fees and balancing his checkbook was just something that Jackie did. It was a instant reflex for her. My husband has been rodeoing his entire life and this was something that she had always done for him. Even when we were dating, it was never that big of a deal to me for Jackie to pay his fees because I didn't feel as if I had "permission" yet, not being his wife. I had made it a "right of passage" in my mind, that when we got married I would take on that role of "financial advisor."

I valued marriage and I was excited to be Cody's wife. I wanted to do it right. I got upset that day because I was only thinking about my perspective—not hers. I accused her of crossing a line that none of us had even talked about. I attacked her character out of frustration for what I interpreted as her not honoring me as his wife. But this bump in the road early on in our marriage only opened up the door for my mind to continue to dwell on other things that I didn't like. I noticed that multiple things would start to bother me. How she called him on the phone every single day. (Something that my family just didn't really do). How he would leave our house in town in the mornings and eat breakfast or get coffee at his parents' house before doing his horse and cattle chores instead of wanting to do that at our house. Or how I felt like Cody expected me to do things exactly how she did them when it came to the house chores or cooking supper, etc. I felt frustrated because I felt so different from her.

I didn't see that as a good thing, obviously. It felt like a bad thing. My MIL is one of the most caring and giving people you will ever meet. She sacrificed so much to care for her family and support her husband. People that know her best know that she is the most selfless and loving person on the planet. I told myself if I wasn't like that, then I must be a bad person. I will never live up to the bar that she set and that made me feel worthless. It also made me feel like an outsider with my husband, like he would always pick his parents over me. I was heavily focused on all of my flaws and was comparing myself against a woman who never set out to make me feel that way but was always just being herself. My insecurities were calling the shots.

Here's what I have learned now several years later (and what I wish I had learned a long time ago). The world is all about competition, but the Kingdom is about collaboration. Solomon says in Ecclesiastes 4:4: *"Then I observed that most people are motivated to success because they envy their neighbors. But this, too, is meaningless-like chasing the wind."* (NLT)

Unhealthy competition is focused on our own insecurities and our own striving for more. We tend to think, if we could just be more like them, maybe then I would be happy. Kingdom collaboration is when: *"Two people are better off than one, for they can help each other succeed. If one person falls, the other can reach out and help. But someone who falls alone is in real trouble."* (Ecclesiastes 4:9-10 NLT) Collaboration means we can learn from each other and help each other grow! In my own brain, I had been creating stories about this competition between me and my MIL (that she didn't even know existed)! I was trying to live up to an ideal that I didn't want for myself and made me frustrated. *I wasn't wired like her, so don't expect me to be her*, I would tell my husband. I felt judged for being different and put up a wall to fully receive her love.

It gave me someone to blame for my unhappiness. It gave me an excuse to be upset. When we point our fingers at other people, it lets us off the hook. That fight I had with my husband about his laundry being all over the floor, that was his mom's fault because she never taught him how to pick up after himself. If only his mom would have taught him how to communicate better, we wouldn't be fighting right now. If only his mom wouldn't have done his checkbook for him, I wouldn't have to be doing it right now. This internal competition I had created was seeping into my marriage because I wanted to be right. I wanted to win. I wanted to find flaws in someone else besides me.

And yes, I was mad at his mom for balancing his checkbook instead of me at the rodeo, but I also was mad at the fact that I had to do it now and my husband wouldn't. One problem turned into another problem. Do you see how irrational that is? I was very hard to please and often heard my husband say, "Nothing is ever good enough for you." Once again, we can see that I was caught up in worldly thinking vs. kingdom thinking. Worldly thinking is all about self. Kingdom thinking is all about how God sees things.

The greatest commandment that we are given is to love God and seek God first. The second is to love others as you love yourself. Matthew 22:36-40 reminds us: *"Teacher, which is the most important commandment in the law of Moses?" Jesus replied, 'You must love the LORD your God with all your heart, all your soul, and all your mind.' This is the first and greatest commandment. A second is equally important: 'Love your neighbor as yourself.' The entire law and all the demands of the prophets are based on these two commandments."* (NLT) So, what does this have to do with your MIL? Well, let's take a closer look at worldly love versus self-love.

10 Things I Hate About My Husband

There are two problems with worldly self-love. Either you have too much of it and you never think about others. It's your way or the highway. You will do whatever you can to get your way and you have a hard time having compassion for others. You can never see someone else's viewpoint. This is obviously a selfish way of thinking. Or, you have absolutely no self-love by the fact that you feel worthless, defeated, or not good enough. You look in the mirror and have no self-respect and you put yourself down with negative words. Because you are miserable with yourself, you make others around you miserable, too.

It's hard to love and serve others when you don't love yourself at all. And when you aren't doing a very good job of loving others, it leads to shame because you know better. Perhaps, you know the greatest commandment like the back of your hand—yet have a hard time living it out. How are we to love others like we love ourselves if our own self-love is completely off?

God is the answer. You seek *His* love. You seek *His* face. You pursue Him so that you can know his true nature and what He says about you. The Bible is not a book of rules; it's a love story, the greatest love story ever told! Everything you read in the Bible, from Genesis to Revelation has God's mercy, grace, and love all wrapped up, showing us the greatest rescue mission of all time, which is saving His children and drawing them nearer to Him.

Jesus is the answer as to why we can live our lives wrapped up safely in God's love and why we can be confident in who He made us to be. When you read the Bible with the intention of learning about God's love and character, instead of what you can find out about yourself and what "not to do," everything changes. When you can see Him as a loving Father, you can start to see yourself as His adored daughter.

The entire Bible is full of scriptures of how much God loves us. Here are just a few:

- *"For the LORD your God is living among you. He is a mighty savior. He will take delight in you with gladness. With his love, he will calm all your fears. He will rejoice over you with joyful songs."* (Zephaniah 3:17)
- *"For the mountains may move and the hills disappear, but even then my faithful love for you will remain. My covenant of blessing will never be broken," says the LORD, who has mercy on you."* (Isaiah 54:10)
- *"But God showed his great love for us by sending Christ to die for us while we were still sinners."* (Romans 5:8)

Once we fully embrace God's overwhelming, abundant, and never-changing love, we can then love others with that same Christ-like love. When we see ourselves the way that God sees us and we actually receive it, we can then see people the way that God sees them too. We can accept the good things about people instead of focusing on the bad.

I'll never forget earlier this year when I looked at myself in the mirror and actually had the thought of *I love myself. I like myself. I am wonderfully and beautifully made.* And I whole-heartedly believed it. I saw myself the way God saw me. I realized that most of the issues I had loving my husband, loving my MIL, and loving other people were not because I was a horribly selfish person; it was because I was in pain. I was an insecure and hurt person, who didn't even love myself. I had been trapped in a shame cycle, never feeling good enough.

If we desire to live out the greatest commandment, which again says: *"You must love the LORD your God with all your heart, all your soul, and all your mind. This is the first and greatest commandment. A second is equally important: "Love your neighbor as yourself."* Then we have to pay attention to the part that says "love your neighbor as yourself!" When I love myself as God loves me, reading His words of adoration in my Bible, reminding myself of who I am to Him, and focusing on seeking Him above all things, everything falls into place. It is easier to love others, provide grace, and hold back judgments and assumptions about the harder relationships in our life. Through this intimacy with God, He also gives us the insights we need about the stories we might be creating in our head around this tough relationship dynamic between us and our MILs.

What are the stories that you are telling yourself about your MIL? Do you really think she's out to make your life miserable and see her son in a broken marriage? Do you really think she is trying to cause you pain by being "too involved" in your son's life? Or could it simply be that calling family members is a normal practice in their family? Could it simply be that the bond she has with her son is very close and she is having a hard time figuring out her new role in your husband's life? (I get this more now being a mom of two boys!) Are you annoyed with the things she didn't teach her son as a child and now you're having to face some challenging conversations with your husband? Is it possible that your MIL did the very best she could with what she had raising her children and that you can honor and respect her for the amazing man you married, despite his flaws?

I believe the answer is yes. As I have stepped into Christ-like love, I am able to appreciate my MIL so much more for the wife, mother, and grandmother that she is. I don't buy into the worldly lie that this MIL/DIL relationship has to be strained and hard or toxic. Even though it may be socially acceptable in your circle of friends to vent and gossip about your MIL, imagine what it will feel like when you focus on collaboration with her instead of competition! Imagine how your marriage will grow as you start to show your husband's mom grace, mercy and love?

I believe there is so much I can learn from Jackie. I believe that despite our differences, we can still work together and understand each other. Our conversations are rich, honest and respected. I believe my life is so much better now that she is part of it. (Plus having her for a neighbor is such a blessing)! Even though Cody and I and our boys are one unit, having a great relationship with Jackie and inviting her into our life doesn't only bless me. It blesses my husband and our boys and it is a freedom that I know you can enjoy, too!

All of this never would have been possible if I had stayed stuck in the stories that I had been telling myself about my MIL. When we stay stuck in judgment of other people and the stories we make up in our minds about them, all we are doing is hurting ourselves. When we hold on to anger or bitterness from past hurt, and we choose not to forgive, we hurt ourselves and ultimately, keeps us separated from resting in our Heavenly Father's perfect love. He is the only one who can give us a perfect love on this side of Heaven. Romans 8:6 tells us: *"So letting your sinful nature control your mind leads to death. But letting the Spirit control your mind leads to life and peace."* (NLT) Set your mind on things above and on God and watch how it changes things!

It would be inconsiderate of me to finish this chapter now without addressing the fact that the issues with your MIL could be more serious than just changing your thoughts and everything will be peachy keen. You may be dealing with someone who is very overbearing, controlling or even manipulative. You may be dealing with a husband who truly is taking his mother's side over you on everything. You may be dealing with a narcissistic personality or someone who isn't acting out of love but is motivated by selfish gain. I do not want to gloss over these hard situations. This is obviously a much bigger issue to tackle and I want to remind you of a few simple truths, not to minimize your pain, but to encourage you to put your hope in Jesus.

- *"For everyone has sinned; we all fall short of God's glorious standard."* (Romans 3:23)
- *"Most important of all, continue to show deep love for each other, for love covers a multitude of sins."* (1 Peter 4:8)
- *"You will bring justice to the orphans and the oppressed, so mere people can no longer terrify them."* (Psalm 10:18)

10 Things I Hate About My Husband

- *"The Lord is more pleased when we do what is right and just than when we offer him sacrifices."* (Proverbs 21:3)

Rest assured, my friend, that God is the One who will right every wrong, not you. So, you can rest easy knowing that it isn't on you to right your MIL's wrongs. It's not on you to try and fix her or change her or even pay for her own wrong-doings. You can trust that God sees your heart in the situation and will protect you.

Of course, you should set the appropriate boundaries and hold people accountable when they are in the wrong. You don't have to put up with destructive motives or behaviors and can look for wisdom in the Word of God on how to do that. But do it out of love, not out of hate. Sometimes taking the time to really understand someone's past can change your perspective on the other person. You learn more about why they are the way they are and why they have the struggles that they have.

As I've talked about extensively in this book, we all have wounds or traumas or beliefs that we have held on to our entire lives. Your MIL is no exception. You may not know the things she has gone through or the guilt she carries. There is pain that motivates her actions and unfortunately, you may be on the receiving end of that pain. Bring that to the Lord and continue to pray for her and harness your authority in the name of Jesus that her heart will be changed.

Other times, a MIL's intentions are most likely not out to harm you—but to protect herself or to fill her own love bucket. It is important to see her as Jesus does and to choose love, even when she does things that you don't always agree with. Maybe she shows her love by buying your kids gifts and it drives you insane because gifts are not your love language. She doesn't do it to create more work for you in organizing all of the toys, she is doing it because that's her love language. It's okay to talk to her about it and set some guidelines but know the underlying reason she does it is because she loves your family so very much. You don't have to agree with everything she does in order to have a healthy relationship with her. When you can be accepting and compassionate towards her, and any other human being for that matter—you are the one that will benefit and change. Life is too short to be hung up on what other people do or don't do.

Acting out of love and compassion is not only what we are called to do as Christ-followers, but it will also gain you favor in your marriage. Proverbs 19:14 reminds us that *"Fathers can give their sons an inheritance of houses and wealth, but only the LORD can give an understanding wife."* (NLT) Oh man, does this give me a boost in holy confidence! I am a gift from God to my husband, so I better start acting like it! When our flesh takes over, we tend to be selfish, hot-tempered, and we adopt a victim mentality. Maybe you are putting your husband in the middle of you and your MIL, asking him to choose. There is competition and your husband's loyalty is being questioned.

How are you approaching the situation? Are you approaching it with understanding or with ultimatums and harsh words? When I think of my own behavior, I think of Proverbs 25:24: *"It's better to live alone in the corner of an attic than with a quarrelsome wife in a lovely home."* Or even better than that is Proverbs 21:19: *"It's better to live alone in the desert than with a quarrelsome, complaining wife."*

Ouch! As much as those verses can sting when we read them, it's true. Sometimes we must stop and acknowledge our words and actions towards our husbands, MIL and other people and choose God's way over our way, even when we don't want to. Especially when we don't want to! It's not easy, and the flesh sometimes does win. But as you are filled with God's love, I promise you that it gets easier. God will make you more holy and righteous as you seek His face and spend time with Him. He will make you more understanding. He imparts to you the fruits of the Holy Spirit. And as he molds you into His beautiful creation, your husband will see it.

10 Things I Hate About My Husband

Many of us aspire to be a Proverbs 31 wife. We desire to be virtuous, trustworthy, good, strong, and helpful. We want our husband to praise us and honor us. We want healthy marriages. But somewhere along the way, we lost ourselves. We adopted an identity apart from God. The enemy used our past traumas and hurts against us and those wounds have poured out into our marriage. We are trying to force ourselves to be a perfect wife and mom. We are pouring from an empty cup. We are full of resentment and find it hard to love. We are wading through life not truly understanding ourselves and who we are in God's eyes and it hurts not just ourselves, but the people in our lives, too.

I hope this book has given you a glimpse into a free and fully alive version of yourself where you don't have to white-knuckle being a Proverbs 31 wife; you just naturally are because of the Holy Spirit living inside of you. Where you don't have to feel shame and condemnation for the mistakes you make, but you know you are saved by Jesus's sacrifice and that the battle you are fighting is already won! Where you can stop trying to love yourself by the world's standards and instead focus on what God says about you and how much He loves you.

I hope you are beginning to realize the power you hold over your thoughts, your beliefs, and your words and that by the authority of Jesus Christ, you don't have to live a life of division and strife amongst those in your life. The enemy can take a backseat and stop his wicked ways of wreaking havoc on your family. You can live a full life of love, not at the expense of yourself but because God's love is your identity. This will not only pour into your husband but into your MIL as well and what a beautiful picture that is to behold.

Yes, your husband left his father and mother to marry you. But as an understanding wife, you can love and accept them just as they are. They can be a healthy extension of your family without tearing your family unit apart. You can set the boundaries with respect and love and be reminded that everyone is doing the best they can with what they have to work with. Your patience and kind conduct will be rewarded and noticed my friend. I promise you, it's worth it.

SCRIPTURE:

Romans 13:8 (NLT)

"Owe nothing to anyone- except for your obligation to love one another. If you love your neighbor, you will fulfill the requirements of God's law."

PRAYER:

Dear Heavenly Father, thank you for the gift of my Mother-in-Law. Thank you for the lessons she teaches me and for the love she has given to my husband. I pray a blessing over her right now and pray that no matter what she is going through, she leans on you. I ask for a healthy and unifying relationship with my Mother-in-Law, despite any past hurts. Help me to have patience and understanding when it comes to this relationship and give me the guidance that I need to work through hard situations and conversations. I desire to be a Proverbs 31 wife and know that I can do it through your love pouring out of me. Amen.

QUESTIONS:

1. Write down the thoughts that you have been believing about your mother-in-law and her behaviors that may annoy you. What perspective shift can you take away from this chapter about that issue?

2. What takeaways did you get from digging into the greatest commandment? How is your own self-worth directly impacting your relationships?

3. Moving forward, what is a goal you have on connecting with your MIL in a new way? Maybe it's improving communication, learning more about her background or even setting a hard boundary on something that truly has gone too far. Whatever it is, have courage as you set out to grow your relationship with the woman who was responsible for bringing your husband into the world! There is so much fruit on the other side of your compassion and love!

12.
Not Tonight.
I Have A Headache.

It's 9:30 pm on a Tuesday night. All the kids are in bed, dishes are in the dishwasher, and the counters are cleared off, finally. You take a minute to actually sit down and realize it was the first time all day that you aren't standing on your feet. Between cooking, working, chauffeuring kids to their activities, and bedtime routines—you have been going pretty hard today. As you finish prepping for the morning, you imagine a bubbly bath and some quiet time may be on the agenda tonight before passing out between the sheets. Just two more quick chores stand in your way between you and your bubbles.

Just as you stand up to start the water for your bath, your husband's eyes connect with you across the room. Like a deer caught in the headlights of a car. *Oh great. I know what that look means. I cannot fathom doing one more "activity" tonight. I just don't have it in me. Here we go again.* And before he can get the words out of his mouth you say, "I can't tonight. I have a headache." As funny as it can be to make jokes about, the fact of the matter is that intimacy in your marriage is a huge deal, a huge struggle, and something not talked about nearly enough! Ladies, our excuses are running out as to why we "can't" anymore and the impact that it is having on our marriage is not something to scoff at. So many issues are at play when our sex lives are less than ideal. Things like pure exhaustion, past traumas or beliefs, societal expectations, and even hormones. Let's dig in a little bit deeper so you can start to connect why you are struggling, how to improve, and the glorious benefits on the other side of having more sex with your husband!

10 Things I Hate About My Husband

It's no secret that God's design for sex in marriage is something that is dramatically misunderstood, ignored, and abused in the world we live in today. From having sex before marriage with multiple people, pornography, or infidelity—sex has become a monster in today's society. It is tossed around so haphazardly and carelessly that no one pays any attention to how very sacred and intentional it is in the context of marriage. Turn on any tv show, movie or pop song, and it is most likely present.

Hit TV shows like "This is Us" and "Yellowstone" fit it in where they can, while other shows like "Outlander" and "Orange is the New Black" are known for their sex scenes. And even though I loved watching Friday Night Lights and One Tree Hill, the fact of the matter is that they make sex seem casual, normal, and as if everyone is doing it. According to the National Institutes of Health "By the exact age of 20 years, 77% of individuals had had sex, and 75% had had sex before marriage; 12% had married." It is everywhere around us, and the world has conditioned us to believe that "it's not that big of a deal" and that "it's what the cool kids are doing."

Except…when you get married. And then it becomes "uncool." Have you ever stopped to consider that? Before you got married, you were tempted beyond belief to have sex before marriage, and maybe you gave in to that temptation. But after marriage all of a sudden it feels like this job we must perform. It becomes less fun, less enticing, and less pleasurable. Why do you think that is?

I love what Mo Isom says in her book *Sex, Jesus, and the Conversations the Church Forgot*: "Because marriage is the enemy's ultimate hunting ground- the greatest revealer of our weaknesses, our struggles, and our insecurities. Satan has no greater victory than seeing a husband and wife break in two. His work started when the words "I do" left your lips. In that breath he was already busy dividing you."

Read that again. The minute you said "I do" the enemy

went to work trying to divide you! And guess where husbands and wives connect in every single aspect—emotionally, mentally, physically and spiritually? You guessed it, in the bedroom. It is the area of your marriage that flies off the hinges faster than you can comprehend because it is the one area that connects the two of you so very much. When we attack the root issues of why you struggle to have sex with your husband, the first thing to consider is the enemy at work.

Because sex is flung around like candy during a parade nowadays, people have no concept of God's intention for it. It wasn't simply to multiply the earth and allow people to have children and reproduce—though that is a major part of it. God created sex to be a beautiful, sacrificial, and pleasurable experience for spouses to draw nearer to each other. It is a gift He gave to us and something to delight in—to enjoy. It is an act of worship and something He designed to unify us in mind, body and spirit.

In marriage, sex is powerful, purposeful and pure. And when we involve God even into this aspect of our lives, He will bless it beyond belief. It's not just the physical act that He will bless. It's the aftermath too. The cuddles and hugs that start to happen more naturally. The eye contact and communication that improves. The way you just feel closer to your husband and how you show up more as a team during the day to day chaos of life. Sex is the ultimate power tool to create oneness in your marriage, so of course the enemy is going to attack it.

In Paul's letter to the Corinthians regarding if it was good to be married, he writes: *"Now regarding the questions you asked in your letter. Yes, it is good to live a celibate life. But because there is so much sexual immorality, each man should have his own wife, and each woman should have her own husband. The husband should fulfill his wife's sexual needs, and the wife should fulfill her husband's needs. The wife gives authority over her body to her husband, and the husband gives authority over his body to his wife. Do not deprive each other of sexual relations, unless you both agree to refrain from sexual intimacy for a limited time so you can give yourselves more completely to prayer. Afterward you should come together again so that Satan won't be able to tempt you because of your lack of self-control.*" 1 Corinthians 7:1-5 (NLT)

Christians in Corinth at this time were surrounded by sexual immorality and sin. It was everywhere! Sound familiar? That's why we need specific instructions from the Lord concerning sex and marriage, not only because of what we are exposed to daily but also because of the natural desires that God has given to us. The study portion of the New Living Translation says: "Marriage provides God's way to satisfy these natural sexual desires and to strengthen the partners against temptation. Married couples have the responsibility to care for each other; therefore, husbands and wives should not withhold themselves sexually from one another but should fulfill each other's needs and desires."

Now, I know what you are thinking. *Sex doesn't satisfy me. I don't get pleasure out of it. My husband only thinks about himself during sex. Sex feels like a job to me. I'm too tired. I want to be intimate in other ways besides just sex.* Girl, listen. I understand! That scene I painted at the beginning of this chapter was describing my life to a T! Sometimes all I want from my husband is for him to leave me alone and stop looking at me like I'm a piece of meat! Ha! Sometimes sex feels like a chore and completely one-sided, but I promise you, it was made for you to enjoy, too.

It starts with your belief and understanding around it. It takes looking at the long term benefits of creating intimacy with your husband vs. the short term repercussions of continuing to put it off. God created sex for you too. It was meant to be desirable and pleasurable for you too. If you currently aren't enjoying it for some reason, that's a problem. And there could be more underlying reasons that you haven't considered yet. I will cover these reasons more in depth later, but there is another belief around sex that I want to address first.

Not only has the world filled our minds with the casualness

of sex, but the church also puts all of the emphasis on the wrongness of sex before marriage. This creates a tidal wave of confusion for Christian women, going back and forth between wanting to succumb to what the world says to "fit in" and then being afraid of sinning against God by premarital sex. When marriage finally does happen, sex still has so many confusing aspects to it for women who don't fully know where they stand on it because there are so many negative associations surrounding it. There may be guilt you are hanging on to from sex before marriage. There may be rooted beliefs about sex being "bad" that you can't get out of your mind, even though you are married. There may be past abuse that you have not truly been healed from yet. All these deeply rooted issues can make their way into the marriage bed and cause you and your husband to struggle to the point where the solution seems to be that you just shouldn't do it at all. It's easier to push it aside instead of facing it head on. But the thing to do most here is to get to the root!

Ask yourself the hard questions about why sex feels uncomfortable for you, why it seems like you always have to talk yourself into it, and possibly what things in your past continue to enter your mind when you are trying to create intimacy with your husband. God's heart is to heal you from any wounds or a "less than perfect" past. I saw a quote one time that said, "Waiting to come to the Lord when you get your life cleaned up is like waiting to go to the ER when you stop bleeding. He doesn't love some future version of you; He loves us in our mess."

And if you think you've created a mess out of your sex life, that's okay! Don't wait to bring your struggles to the Lord. He will meet you right where you are. His heart is to heal and set you free so you can enjoy intimacy with your husband. You can enjoy the connection that it brings not only in the bedroom, but in your everyday moments with your man, too!

I've heard this phrase multiple times from different faith mentors and each time it strengthens my fight against the enemy's attacks—especially when it comes to sex. "Sex is the ultimate middle finger to sin and to the devil." I mean, for real! Sex was created by our Creator as a way to connect husbands and wives emotionally, mentally, spiritually and physically. When used correctly in marriage, with both spouses caring for each other, it gives the message to Satan that nothing can divide you and that your hearts are together—not divided. With that frame of mind, it's a lot easier to remember who the enemy is. And it isn't your husband.

However, one of the most common complaints of women who are having issues in the bedroom is that their love tank is empty, so they have nothing left to give. If you aren't feeling loved by your husband in other ways and you feel depleted, of course you won't feel like giving your husband what you think he "needs." *If he's not helping me with the dishes tonight, he ain't getting lucky*, you think to yourself. Which then becomes a test that your husband has to pass. *I don't know the last time he said something sweet to me... so why would I want to have sex with him?* you think to yourself for the 19th time this week, while you brush off his advances once again because the thought of it makes your skin crawl. It is the classic case of love tanks not being filled which leads to depriving the other of an essential need. And as someone who operated with those thoughts myself, I can attest that it only continued to divide us instead of bringing us closer together.

Remember where those dividing thoughts come from. God is not telling you to test your husband and to only give him sex when you think he deserves it. 1 John 4:19-21 says: "*We love each other because he loved us first. If someone says, "I love God," but hates a Christian brother or sister, that person is a liar; for if we don't love people we can see, how can we love God, whom we cannot see? And he has given us this command: Those who love God must also love their Christian brothers and sisters.*" (NLT)

This includes our husbands, ladies! I'm not saying this to

condemn you and I'm not telling you to just jump in bed every time your husband wants it. But marriage is sacrificial. Marriage will make you more holy and righteous when you put God first. Marriage is laying down your life for another and putting someone else's needs above your own. Remembering who the enemy is in your marriage will absolutely change the game for you. Seeking God's love and understanding your true identity as a daughter of God will fill you with love that overflows out of you onto your husband.

Sex does not have to be this game you play with your husband. It is not a weapon! Sex can and will be something that unifies you, connects you, and strengthens your marriage more than almost anything else. And you should be open and honest with your spouse about it. Talk to him about your needs and desires. Let him know that you also want to be intimate outside of the bedroom and look for ways to express that. Date nights, movie nights, hugs and kisses, and understanding each other's love languages are all ways to be intimate beyond sex too. It takes work and communication to get to a place of give and take.

Your sex life does not have to be perfect. It is for the two of you and that's it. It does not have to be like the movies. Some nights it may be romantic, some nights it may be fast. Some nights might be planned, other nights may be spontaneous. That's the beauty of it. When you face your past, heal your heart, draw closer to God, and understand the true purpose of sex in marriage, it will restore what the enemy has tried to take from you.

Life is full of seasons. It's full of twists and turns that can seriously disrupt your regularly scheduled programming (if you know what I mean)! Things like having a baby, postpartum season, moving to a new house or switching jobs, or facing really challenging things like the death of a loved one. It is understandable that your sex life would take a back seat during these times. But I challenge you to not let it slip. I challenge you to keep open lines of communication with your husband going so he can understand not only you and your needs better, but the value that you put on your sex life. This has been a huge positive in my own marriage. Reminding my husband that I do value him and care about our sex life, even if it's "that time of the month" allows us to still keep some sort of flame burning!

Understanding my natural hormone cycle and how that plays a part in my desire for sex has been extremely helpful with our physical intimacy. Not sure why it took me 30 years to understand that I have hormones and they affect me, but here we are! I'm no expert, but there is a very real discrepancy between a woman's desire and a man's desire and we would be silly to not acknowledge that. There is a reason why it seems like men are ready to do it at all times of the day and women can really struggle

Let's unpack it in layman's terms. During the course of a month, a woman will go through four different hormone cycles. And the more you can track your cycle and understand your body and how you are feeling, the more you can communicate that with your spouse, which hopefully leads to him showing you more grace when you are extra cranky and moody.

Week one is period week. In the beginning, estrogen levels are low so you may be more tired, achy and cranky along with other period symptoms. Towards the end of the week, estrogen levels are rising which will help your mood and physical strength. Chocolate is most likely what is on your mind and literally nothing else. During week two, your estrogen levels are rising even more which increases your energy and mood. You may feel more confident and attractive and even have a glow about you! This is the week that I make the best content for my social media platforms and feel like I can literally conquer the world as a wife, mom and business owner. As you approach ovulation, your libido is increasing which is obviously something that hubby is excited about and it's time for some one-on-one! After ovulation in week three, estrogen falls and progesterone rises. This means you may feel more emotional this week and find yourself eating for two because you are in between ovulation and menstruation and your body is preparing for a possible pregnancy. Even though your libido is dropping, you may still desire to feel emotionally close to your spouse. And finally, in week four, estrogen is plunging and with it, your mood. PMS symptoms raise their ugly head and it's important to pay attention to your nutrition and lifestyle even more if you do have intense symptoms vs. mild ones.

When men say women are complicated—they can blame our hormones for that! This is a natural occurrence that we have to deal with literally every single month and it can be exhausting. I'm not saying to plan your entire life around your hormones, but definitely use them to your advantage when you can and give yourself grace when you notice your emotions seem to be all over the place. Don't try to white-knuckle intimacy when you are literally in battle with your hormones. Share these things with your husband and give him the chance to show up with a chocolate bar when you need it. Give him a heads-up as to why you know you won't be in the mood on Friday, but you would still like to spend time with him in other ways. Again, understanding your hormones is not something to use as another excuse to create division between you—but to increase the connection overall. It's time to stop playing the shame game as to why you "aren't in the mood" and to start understanding your body more and taking better care of it!

SIDE NOTE: If you have a feeling that hormones are affecting either you or your husband in a negative way, I recommend getting your hormones checked and looking into natural remedies to help balance your body to its natural state. We are exposed to many hormone disruptors daily and it's absolutely possible that this is affecting your sex life on a natural level (not a spiritual level). For more information on my favorite hormone supplements, check out the reference page at the end of this book and visit femsense.com for even more information on tracking your cycle!

10 Things I Hate About My Husband

When it comes down to it, what lies could you be believing about your sex life with your husband? Do you believe that you aren't desirable? Do you believe that you just don't need it? Do you believe that your husband just doesn't understand you? Do you believe that it's just been too long and you aren't sure how to get this part of your marriage back? Maybe trust has been broken and you are struggling in the hurt of the aftermath.

Whatever it is, you can lay those thoughts at the feet of Jesus. Allow Him to heal your heart and expose the lies. Allow Him to show you what it feels like to be loved and to love. This may be an area of your marriage that really needs some work and that's ok. Give you and your husband grace and patience as you navigate this intimate and holy act. By the power of the blood of Jesus, you are not bound to living in fear, doubt, worry, lies, or hurt. You are set free, which means free to experience connection with your husband the way that God intended it, not as the world does.

Sex in your marriage is a weapon against Satan's attacks. Sex in your marriage unifies and connects. Sex is a gift from God himself for the both of you. It's time to make it a priority in your marriage and see the fruit of what it can do!

DISCLAIMER: This chapter is not intended for the woman in an abusive or manipulative relationship, where the man is controlling or toxic in any way. God calls husbands to love their wives the way that Christ loves the church (Ephesians 5:25). **If sex is being used against you instead of *for* you, I want to encourage you to seek help. The National Domestic Violence Hotline is 800-799-7233 or seek local help at your church or community centers.**

Shayla Huber

SCRIPTURE:

Romans 12:9-10 (NLT)

"Don't just pretend to love others. Really love them. Hate what is wrong. Hold tightly to what is good. Love each other with genuine affection and take delight in honoring each other."

PRAYER:

Father God, thank you for the gift of sex. Thank you for the gift of my husband. Please continue to teach me and show me how to love my husband in this way. Please restore what has been lost and help us move forward in this area of our marriage. Show me the areas of my heart that need healing and create in me a pure heart. As I pursue loving you more, let that love overflow to my husband. Bond our hearts together and show us what it means to live as one. I also declare protection from all attacks of the enemy in Jesus' name. Because of the price Jesus paid, I am set free and desire to bring glory and honor to you in all areas of my life and marriage, including this one. I love you Abba. Amen.

QUESTIONS:

1. How do you normally react when your husband wants to have sex? Where do your thoughts go and are you noticing that you are playing the back and forth game with him?
2. Are there hurts or wounds from your past that came up for you in this chapter? Ask God to continue to reveal what needs to be healed. This includes any sexual sin and/or guilt you may be holding on to.
3. How will tracking your hormones help you in the long run when it comes to creating intimacy with your husband? In what other ways can you improve communication with your husband to create that connection and deeper intimacy?

13.
Where Does Your Wealth Lie?

"At its heart, marriage is more than a man and woman falling in love and spending life together. God has many priceless purposes for marriage. He created it to eliminate loneliness through companionship, multiply our effectiveness through teamwork, and mature us into Christlikeness. He designed marriage to guard our purity through sexual fulfillment, grow families through procreation, and bring about the enjoyment of walking in love and oneness. But God's ultimate purpose for marriage is a hidden mystery that is greater than all of these combined. God masterfully orchestrated marriage to reveal the beauty of His glory.

In fact, each of His purposes for marriage reveals a characteristic of God in eternity. Our oneness and companionship reflect His union in the Trinity. Our purity honors His holiness. Our procreation reflects Him as Creator of life. Our love is founded in the truth that God is love. And our love provides a living portrait of the gospel- Christ's unconditional love for His people, His church, His bride (Revelation 21:9). Your marriage is a mystery revealing His majesty." (Excerpt from: *The Love Dare Devotional*, Day 21.)

I have spent the last 12 chapters digging into all the ways that I struggled in my marriage. The ways I hated my husband. And ultimately, all of the ways that the enemy tried to destroy my marriage. All the lies that I believed and unhealed wounds I had dictated how I showed up in my marriage.

My hope and prayer is that your eyes have been opened to God's love through these pages. That you can now see yourself the way that God sees you. And that as part of God's family, your life and marriage is designed to thrive, not just survive. No matter the circumstance, hurt, distance, or brokenness, God can restore you and your husband. "*I have swept away your sins like a cloud. I have scattered your offenses like the morning mist. Oh, return to me, for I have paid the price to set you free.*" (Isaiah 44:22 NLT). Oh, how freeing it is to be a daughter of God and to believe in His promises for our life!

Sister, you are loved. You are chosen and redeemed. What Jesus did on the cross for us is sometimes too much to comprehend and understand, but it's been paid in full. You are saved the minute you accept Jesus Christ into your heart as your Lord and Savior. You don't have to look back any more at your mistakes. You don't have to live with shame and condemnation. You can look forward to a full life, filled with God's love.

Run, don't walk after God. Ask Him to heal your heart, make it new, forgive you, and lead you every day of your life. You may think putting God first and taking your focus off of your husband would potentially do more harm than good—false. The more you pursue God and allow His love to fill you to overflowing, the more your marriage will grow. The closer you get to the One who created marriage, the more you will be like Him and love your husband like He does.

Friend, I was a woman who married the love of her life. Who married a great man, and yes, an imperfect one, too. I married a man who I loved, but I wanted him to save me from myself. I wanted him to love me so perfectly that I never had to worry again. And despite all of his efforts to do so, he failed. Because God never intended for him to be my savior. I already had a savior, and His name is Jesus Christ. He is the only one who can save us from our pain, our hurts, our sins, and our insecurities. Once you put Him back in his rightful place as first in your life, everything will change. Your husband does have an important part in your life as your companion, partner, spouse, and lover; but he was never supposed to be your savior. No human was meant to do that for another. My husband does not complete me; he compliments me. Let this revelation free you and change you. Let it give you confidence as you continue to fight the good fight for your marriage with God as your guide and leader.

You are never alone in this and I pray that as God molds you into who you were always meant to be, your husband joins you and you will completely live out Matthew 19:6 which says: *"Since they are no longer two but one, let no one split apart what God has joined together."*

Remember the story of the lame man by the pool of Bethesda? In Luke 5:7, the lame man responds to Jesus when he asks him if he would like to get well after being sick for 38 years... *"I can't, sir,"* the sick man said, *"for I have no one to put me into the pool when the water bubbles up. Someone else always gets there ahead of me."* But in verse 8 Jesus told him: *"Stand up, pick up your mat, and walk!"*

God calls us to be active participants in our healing journey. He is our ultimate healer—we don't have to wait for anyone else to help us. The lame man waited for 38 years for someone to pick him up and put him in the pool and if it wasn't for Jesus coming to say "get up!" he probably would have waited his entire life, instead of actually living! Jesus died on the cross to give us a blessed life, not a cursed life. He died for us to give us freedom and abundance and a life lived with Him. Your marriage is a beautiful story being written. Invite God back into it and see what He can do.

The other night, I was rereading an amazing book called *Loving Him Well*. I had read it three years ago, when I started on my journey of improving my marriage. I took many strategies from the book and implemented them and can honestly say that our marriage improved over the last three years. It was a good start. Loving my husband in his love language, trying to not take things so personal when my husband was having a bad day, and improving my work/family balance were things I worked on in order to help my marriage grow. But as I read the book this time all the way through, it was as if my soul connected with it in a whole new way. As Gary Thomas, the author, was talking about God's love being the ultimate validation and protection that we need and that we can influence our husband through that lens, it hit me that by God truly healing my heart this year, I was able to see the benefits in my marriage by seeking God's love first.

Three years ago, my soul wasn't prepared for that. Three years ago, I still had an orphan spirit and was going about life my own way. Three years ago, I had an unhealed heart, with wounds I didn't want to face. The words on the page were helpful and encouraging, but they did not take away the bitterness and resentment I had in my heart. They did not solve all of my problems in my marriage or my life.

But reading those words now—it brings the purpose of this book full circle. Because as I wrote this book for you, God healed my heart for me. Healing my heart was the missing link to ultimate transformation and freedom. Talking about God's love is one thing. But feeling His love is an entirely different thing. Religion says that we have to change for God to love us, but the Gospel says that His love changes us. I pray that as you embark on a healing journey of your own (which is not an overnight process, mind you), you can remember that all roads lead back to Jesus. His work is finished and the Holy Spirit is at work inside of you.

God has a plan and a purpose for you and the work you are doing on your own growth will benefit not only your husband, but your children and your children's children and all generations to come. Seek out the help you need through therapy or coaching, surround yourself with likeminded Christian women who will pray with you and encourage you, and seek God's heart above all else and watch what He will do in your life!

"In the twelfth century, the vast wealth of Weinsberg Castle in Germany made it a jewel just waiting to be taken. Enemy forces besieged the stone fortress and threatened the riches within.

The inhabitants stood no chance of defending themselves against such a great horde, and the opposing marauders demanded a complete surrender. If the occupants would agree to give up their wealth and the men would give up their lives, the women and children would be spared. After consultation, the women of Weinsberg Castle asked for one provision: to leave with as many possessions as they could carry. If the opposing forces would agree to this one request, the men inside would lay down their arms and hand over the castle's riches. Fully aware of the wealth of riches loaded within the castle, the enemy forces agreed. After all, how much could these women take? Finally, the castle gates opened, and the sight that emerged elicited tears from even the most calloused soldiers. *Every woman carried her husband on her back.* How many of those rescued men were perfect? Not one. But every one of those imperfect men meant more to their wives than anything they owned. Where is your greatest wealth?" (Excerpt from *Loving Him Well*, by Gary Thomas.)

Where is your greatest wealth? I know full well, if I was a woman in that castle, I would have chosen the same thing. My husband is my greatest gift here on earth. My partner in this life and someone who has shown me love and grace when I didn't deserve it. Someone who stuck by me when things looked dark or when he didn't understand what I was going through. He is my greatest treasure because no amount of money or success could ever replace the fruit that our marriage produces, simply because we now love each other as God calls us to love. Marriage will always be a work in progress. Two imperfect people choosing to never give up on each other. But I promise you, with God leading the way, it is a lot easier! With God leading the way, the enemy's tactics are weak and powerless.

With God leading the way, there is freedom!

10 Things I Hate About My Husband

SCRIPTURE:

Matthew 19:6 NLT

"Since they are no longer two but one, let no one split apart what God has joined together."

PRAYER:

Dear Heavenly Father, thank you for the treasure that is my husband. Thank you for opening up my eyes to the true gift that marriage is. Thank you for meeting me right where I am on this journey called life. I am excited to be on this healing journey with you. I am trusting in your overwhelming power to help me break free from the strongholds in my life. I am believing in restoration for my marriage and the plan you have for me. Thank you for all of the blessings you have given me and will continue to give. Through your love, I am set free. I love you! Amen!

EPILOGUE
10 Things I Love About My Husband

It's not every day that your wife comes to you and shares a book idea titled *10 Things I Hate About My Husband.* The fact of the matter is that Cody could have said no. He could have been too uncomfortable with it. He could have been the one to encourage me to keep it to myself. But he didn't. And that's the first thing that I love about him. Please read along as I honor my husband in this very long and probably overdone epilogue.

1. **Cody**. I love that you encourage me in everything I set out to do, even when you don't fully understand it. I love that when I was filled with doubts, you reminded me that if God asked me to do this, then I needed to do it. Thank you for being my biggest cheerleader and encouragement on this project, that not only will bring healing to other women, but that brought healing to me.

2. **I love your patience.** God knew I needed a patient man to deal with my heart, and that's why He sent me you. When I was overcome with impatience and frustration, you were the calm to my storm. When I needed to be reminded of humble beginnings, you were there. Thank you for being a model of patience when I needed it most, not only during the writing of this book but in our day to day life.

3. **I love your work ethic.** I love your passion and vigor for roping and the leather shop. I love that you have created a living around your talents, skills, and interests and made it into something for all of us to enjoy. I love that you never quit and look for ways to

improve. Thank you for bringing me into this life of freedom, craziness, and entrepreneurship and showing me a life beyond what everyone else is doing.

4. **I love that you don't care about what others think.** As a recovering people pleaser, it is a quality that has always intrigued me about you and I've always admired it so much. You are who you are and you make no apologies for it. And even though I've stumbled in this area, you always were there, loving me and accepting me in all my stages and insecurities. And I love that now that I found my true identity in Christ, it has only brought us closer together. Praise Him who makes all things new!

5. **I love that you resemble Jesus in so many ways.** You are always there to lend a helping hand to someone in need. You are generous and kind. You are giving of your time and resources. You are selfless and compassionate. You would do anything for your family. You have a pure heart and I know God is continuing to work in you every single day.

6. **I love that you are a great dad.** We are raising two very unique, special, and wonderful boys and to see them with you brings me more joy than I can express. Thank you for taking this job as dad seriously and for giving Leroy and Wacey something to model. You are their closest view of God here on earth, and to show love and validation to them means so much. Thank you for being my partner in parenthood.

7. **I love that you are affectionate and pursue me.** Some days I don't understand what you see in me when I'm in my sweats and a messy ponytail, but somehow you still make me feel beautiful. I love that you value our intimate life in a way that not only benefits you, but me too. I just love that you love me.

8. **I love your honesty.** Even when you have to make a hard phone call or decision, you always do what is

right. People can count on you to tell the truth, no matter what. I love that I can count on you to be honest with me, even when you give me truths I don't want to hear.

9. **I love that you like spending time with me.** I love that you care about me watching you rope or riding in the ranger to check cows. I love that you care about taking me out on dates and making me feel loved. I love that my presence is enough for you and that you don't expect me to be anything but who I am. I love spending time with you and honoring our family above other worldly things.

10. **I love that you love God.** I love that as I drew nearer to Him, you did too. I love that my relationship with Him did not make you jealous or resentful. I'm so thankful that through God's love, we have a new marriage and future. I love that our dreams are aligning again and that God's blessings are with us every day. Through the ups and the downs, we can call on Him to guide us every step of the way.

I love you, Cody Huber! You are my treasure and I am so thankful to be doing this life with you. I thank God everyday for you and our story and would not change a single thing about any of it. Thank you for letting me share it with the world!

Always and Forever,
Shayla

NOTES

NOTES

NOTES

Prayer to Renounce the Orphan Spirit

This is the prayer I prayed while learning more about the orphan spirit and making the decision to allow God to heal that part of my life. I encourage you to pray this prayer as well to help you in your journey.

Abba, thank you for being my father. I invite you to heal the orphan mindsets that I may have. My only desire is to confidently approach you in intimacy. Thank you for always paving a way for us to be close Oh Lord. You are so good. You saw the gold in me when I couldn't even see me. I'm learning to love who I am because you're a good teacher. You are the potter and I am your unique and beautiful masterpiece. I'm thankful that you created me the way I am. And I'm grateful for the gift of the Holy Spirit to keep me in purity and connection with you.

I am in love with the way that you guide, protect, teach, discipline, and bless me papa. I rejoice because I am learning how much you love me more and more every day. I'm learning more and more that everything you do is motivated by love. I hope to be more and more like you. Papa, set my heart a blaze for all the fatherless and motherless in the world. I want to help others to see the beauty of intimacy with you. At your word rejection, pride, fear, doubt, unworthiness, and lack are defeated. And I'm excited because your lost children will rejoice when they understand this GOOD NEWS. I love you Abba. Amen.

REFERENCES

Chapman, Gary. (2015). *The 5 Love Languages: The Secret to Love That Lasts*. Northfield Publishing.

Finer, Lawrence B., PhD. (2007). "Trends in Premarital Sex in the United States, 1954-2003." Public Health Reports. Retrieved from: https://www.ncbi.nlm.nih.gov/pmc/articles/PMC1802108/ (pg.174)

Hetland, Leif. (2020). *The Orphan Spirit*. Convergence Press.

Isom, Mo. (2018). *Sex, Jesus, and the Conversations the Church Forgot*. Baker Books.

Garcia, Karrie. (2023). *Free and Fully Alive*. Zondervan Press.

Kendrick, Alex & Stephen. (2013). *The Love Dare Day by Day: A Year of Devotions for Couples*. B&H Books.

Leman, Dr. Kevin. (2006). *Sex Begins in the Kitchen: Creating Intimacy to Make Your Marriage Sizzle.* Revell Publishing.

Daniels, Christina. (2022.) Orphan Spirit prayer. Adorned Heart.com. Retrieved from: https://www.adornedheart.com/what-is-an-orphan-spirit-characteristics/#Prayer_to_Renounce_the_Orphan_Spirit

SeekUnited.Org. (2020). "What is Stress Resilience?" Retrieved from: https://www.seekunited.org/wellness/stress-resilience#:~:text=What%20Is%20Stress%20Resilience%3F,way%20you%20respond%20that%27s%20important (pg.61)

Thomas, Gary. (2018). *Loving Him Well*. Zondervan Press.

Wilkinson, Bruce. (2005). *The Prayer of Jabez: Breaking Through to the Blessed Life.* Multnomah Publishing.

10 Things I Hate About My Husband

The Happy Juice I talked about in Chapter 4 and the Amare Ignite supplements I talked about in Chapter 12 helped me feel like myself again and they're all natural! I wanted to share them with you all, so click the QR code below to try some for yourself!

 CHAPTER 4- HAPPY JUICE

 CHAPTER 12- HORMONE HELP

Acknowledgements

My Heavenly Father: Your love is the greatest, most magnificent love I have ever felt in this life and I will spend the rest of my days sharing it with others. Thank you for this dream and for giving me the strength to pursue it. Thank you for the calling you have given me to speak into women's lives, help families flourish, and bring them closer to you. I always knew you had a purpose for me and this one is beyond my wildest imagination. Your patience, forgiveness, mercy, grace, and love are truly all I need and I will praise your name again and again, throughout eternity. I love being your daughter and I love you with all of my heart.

Cody: Thank you for being patient, supportive, and encouraging throughout the conception, writing, and release of this book! Thank you for building me up when fear, doubt, and worry tried to stop me from sharing our story. We are living out God's promise of being a team and we make a pretty good one! I love you more today than I did when we first got married and cherish the life we are building together. Your love is truly heaven sent and I can't wait to see what God has in store for us next! I love you, Babe!

Mom: You've always been my biggest cheerleader, and this project did not change that. Thank you for being a sounding board during this process and encouraging me to keep leaning into God's wisdom for truth. I would not be the woman I am today without your love and support my entire life and I am forever grateful for you. Our story hasn't been the easiest one, but God has been there the entire time, shifting every puzzle piece together. I pray you know how truly special you are to me, as my mom, best friend, and confidant. I love you!

10 Things I Hate About My Husband

Jackie: Not many daughter-in-laws write a book about how much they hate their husbands, but yours does! I'll never forget the fear I had telling you about this book, and how you so lovingly embraced it. God blessed me immensely when He gave me you as a mother-in-law and I'm so thankful for our relationship and the way it has grown. You raised my favorite person in all the world and we would not be able to pursue our dreams without you. You are the best neighbor ever and I thank you in advance for all of the times I will continue sending the boys up to you to grab sugar or flour. You are the best; Jack and I love you!

Stephanie: Stephanie, this book would not be what it is without you! I still can't believe the clarity, creativity, and stories that came out of me from our sessions together. I hope you know how much healing God brought me from us working together on this book and how your encouragement about sharing this message kept me going. I needed an editor that saw my vision, my heart, and God's ultimate purpose with this book and you were the perfect person for the job! Thank you for walking alongside me as I officially become a published author. Your insights, friendship, and prayers mean the world to me!

Cassie: Four years ago, I was a lost, broken down, and empty version of Shayla. You took the very last flame I had in me and saw the potential of what it could become. Working with you and Amare changed the trajectory of my entire life. Thank you for seeing me before I really saw me. Thank you for not letting me stay stuck in a life that was not God's best for me. Thank you for encouraging me to pick up that first book on marriage and for encouraging me to heal my heart. Your guidance, friendship, and support has led me to this place and I cannot thank God enough for how, when, and where He placed you in my life. His divine timing is perfect. I love you so very much!

Heather: I'll never forget the question you asked me before we even started working together. "How do you think I can help you?" And as I burst into tears, I just knew you were going to unlock something in me that God was trying to get out. We didn't know it at the time, but this book was it. I don't have the words to describe what you have done for me. Thank you for being obedient to God's calling on your life to help women like me rest in their true identity in Christ and fulfill their Kingdom purpose. I am who I am today because of the prophetic words you have spoken over my life. Your prayers, coaching, and encouragement are filled with the Holy Spirit and I can't wait to see where we go next!

Caitlin: God's divine timing is so great and I couldn't finish this book without giving you, my new sister in Christ, a shout-out. From day one of our friendship, you just got me. Thank you for sharing your visions, dreams, and encouragement with me. Thank you for putting your eyes on this book and boosting it with the best analogies. Thank you for listening to me cry, laugh, scream, and freak out every step of this journey. Your belief in me, in this message, and in God's hand helped me tremendously during this process and I can't thank you enough, my friend! Here is to becoming published authors together, while we shout His name on high!

Kristen: Oh, my sweet Kristen. Where do I even begin? Through many ups and downs, you have been a constant friend, unofficial virtual assistant, and teammate. We've seen each other at our lowest of lows and highest of highs and we've both grown so much over the past few years. Thank you for the work you have done on my website, in my membership group, and for being the one to always step in and say, "let me help you!" I truly don't know what I would do without you. Everyone needs a Kristen in their life, but they can't have mine!

10 Things I Hate About My Husband

Shelby and Chelsia: Many people don't see the behind-the-scenes work or pay much attention to what goes into the making of a book... but now I do! Shelby, I chose you to create my cover based on the fact that you love Jesus. I wasn't aware of your talent, skills, or background... but I trusted that you would produce something beautiful simply because of who you are. I'm so glad I did! Thank you for your work on the cover art and bringing my vision, personality, and boldness of this message to life! It is perfect! I appreciate you more than you know!

And Chelsia, from the minute I talked with you, I knew I needed you in my life! One more person in my corner to say, "Shayla, so many wives need this book." Thank you for believing in what I'm doing and for your work on the editing and formatting. You are a gift from the Lord!

Family and Friends: Lastly, to the numerous friends and family in my corner who have supported me, prayed for me, and shared my message with others. Thank you. It has not been easy to expose the ugliest pieces of who I used to be. How blessed am I to have so many wonderful people in my life that said, "When God calls you to it, He will see you through it." I have felt the support, prayers and love more than I can express!

About the Author

Shayla is a rodeo wife to Cody, boy mom to Leroy and Wacey and they live in Iowa on their family farm. She is passionate about helping women discover their true identity in Christ in order to help marriages and families flourish.

For more information on connecting with Shayla, visit her website: www.shaylamariehuber.com or follow her account on TikTok @shaylahuber30!

10 Things I Hate About My Husband is her first book.

Made in the USA
Middletown, DE
06 September 2024

60138914R00110